THE REAL READER'S QUART.

Slightly Foxed

'A Separate World'

NO.67 AUTUMN 2020

Cover illustration: Tor Falcon, 'Fox's Earth in Calveley Hall Wood', pastel

Tor Falcon is an artist who walks and makes drawings on her journeys through the landscape. Past projects include the Peddars Way and the South Downs. Her most recent project, to follow, draw and write about the rivers of Norfolk, took four years to complete. A hundred of the resulting drawings were exhibited at Norwich Castle Museum and then at Abbott & Holder in London. For more of her work visit www.torfalcon.co.uk.

Design by Octavius Murray

Layout by Andrew Evans

Colophon and tailpiece by David Eccles

Published by Slightly Foxed Limited
53 Hoxton Square
London N1 6PB

tel 020 7033 0258
email office@foxedquarterly.com
www.foxedquarterly.com

Slightly Foxed is published quarterly in early March, June, September and December

Annual subscription rates (4 issues)
UK and Ireland £48; Overseas £56

Single copies of this issue can be bought for £12.50 (UK) or £14.50 (Overseas)

All back issues in printed form are also available

ISBN 978-1-910898-47-5
ISSN 1742-5794

Printed and bound by Smith Settle, Yeadon, West Yorkshire

Contents

Contents

The Slightly Foxed Podcast

A new episode of our podcast is available on the 15th of every month. To listen, visit www.foxedquarterly.com/pod or search for Slightly Foxed on Audioboom, iTunes or your podcast app.

Subscriber Benefits

Slightly Foxed can obtain any books reviewed in this issue, whether new or second-hand. To enquire about a book, to access the digital edition of *Slightly Foxed* or to view a list of membership benefits, visit www.foxedquarterly.com/members or contact the office: 020 7033 0258/office@foxedquarterly.com.

From the Editors

There's a fox's earth on the cover of this issue, but thanks in large part to you, this Fox has far from gone to earth. We've loved receiving your encouraging messages and emails during this difficult year, and you've pulled out all the stops with extra purchases, subscriptions and renewals. 'I read *Slightly Foxed* in bed with my morning tea as an antidote to the news,' writes N. Reifler. Now it's autumn, and we're happy to say that our publishing programme is up and running, with a great deal to look forward to.

There are two new Cubs to add to *The Eagle of the Ninth* and *The Silver Branch*, the first two in Rosemary Sutcliff's series of Roman novels, which we reissued last year. *Frontier Wolf* and *The Lantern Bearers* (see p. 41) take the story of the Roman occupation of Britain through its twilight years, to the moment when the last of the Legions departs, leaving Britain at the mercy of warring tribes and Saxon invaders. Like all the best books, they make you long for more, and fortunately there are three more to come. These take the story of Britain through the Dark Ages to the Norman Conquest, and we'll be publishing them next year.

This season's Slightly Foxed Edition is Jessica Mitford's *Hons and Rebels*. It's the story of the Mitford who got away, the one who grew up despising her aristocratic roots and her deeply conservative upbringing, became a socialist, eloped with her cousin and ended up in the USA on the eve of the Second World War, where she remained, espousing left-wing causes, and writing critically about America. Her account of her eccentric upbringing as one of the six headstrong Mitford sisters is brilliantly funny, but there's a strong undertone of tragedy in it too. Nancy Mitford's biographer Selina Hastings writes about it on p. 13.

Then there's an extra treat coming at the end of September – *An Englishman's Commonplace Book* compiled by Roger Hudson from material he's collected over the past forty years. Ranging over the centuries, it's a rich collection of arresting facts, vivid descriptions, absurd observations and wise words put together by a well-read man with a sharp eye and an ironic – and indeed very English – sense of humour. It's not just a book for Christmas but a book for the times, one that gives us a perspective on our own history. A perfect present for a thoughtful and humorous friend, and a must-have addition to your own bedside table or spare-room shelf.

And finally another story that demonstrates again how wonderful and unusual *Slightly Foxed* readers are. Last autumn we received a letter from a subscriber, enclosing a cheque for £500. It was to spend in any way we chose that would make our office life easier, she said, a thank-you for what we do. After much thought we decided we'd like to spend her generous present on something more lasting than a new coffee-machine or photocopier and you'll find the elegant result on p. 18. It's the new Slightly Foxed bookplate, commissioned from the illustrator and printmaker Clare Curtis, who did the cover illustration for Issue 56. This is a generic bookplate which leaves space for you to write your own name rather than having it individually printed, which at £10 (plus p&p) for a hundred cuts the cost considerably. We love it, and hope you will too.

GAIL PIRKIS & HAZEL WOOD

John Watson

A Separate World

IAN THOMSON

When I think back to that first visit of mine to Estonia in 1988, I see muted, metallic-grey tones of fog and sea; above all I remember a sense of wonder that I was finally on my way to my mother's homeland. Ingrid was 17 when, stateless and displaced, she arrived in England in 1947, having fled westwards from the Baltic ahead of Stalin's advancing Red Army. She had not been back to her native land since. Now, half a century later, I was sailing to the Estonian capital of Tallinn from Helsinki – a three-hour journey by ferry across the Gulf of Finland. The *Independent Magazine* had asked me to report on Moscow's waning power in the Soviet Baltic. A hammer and sickle flapped red from the ship's stern as we set sail. The air was pungent with engine oil as I walked towards the stern and watched Helsinki's Eastern Orthodox cathedral dwindle to a dot.

On the flight over to Helsinki from London I had read a novel by the Estonian writer Jaan Kross, *Four Monologues on St George.* It investigates the life of the Tallinn-born artist Michel Sittow, who had worked as court painter to Queen Isabella of Spain in the late fifteenth century, and it had been published in Moscow in 1982 in a translation by Robert Dalglish. I did not know it then, but Kross had written sixteen other semi-factual historical novels set in Estonia under the Swedish, Danish, Russian and Nazi occupations. The novels all sought to outwit Soviet censorship – 'writing between the

---

Jaan Kross, *The Czar's Madman* (1978: English trans. 1992) and *The Conspiracy and Other Stories* (1988: English trans. 1995) are both available in paperback from Harvill.

lines', Kross called it – and use history as a way to restore Estonia's national memory under dictatorship and confirm the country's place as Europe's ultimate East-West borderland.

In the centuries before Kross, Western travellers had marvelled at the untranslatable names and the 'exotic' strangeness of sea-girt Estonia. In 1839 Lady Elizabeth Eastlake (later notorious for her hostile review of *Jane Eyre* in the *Quarterly Review*) had travelled by sledge across the country to a chorus of howling wolves. Estonia was viewed in Eastlake's day (and to an extent, it still is) as a Ruritanian outpost as remote and exotic as the fictional Syldavia of the Tintin books. (The eye-patch-wearing pilot Piotr Skut of Tintin's *Flight 714 to Sydney* actually is Estonian.) In Kross's view, foreign deprecations of the Baltic as a notional 'Dracula-Land' on the fringes of Eurasia are mostly born of ignorance.

*

A Russian voice over the ship's tannoy cautioned us to put our watches forward by an hour in anticipation of the Soviet time zone. Presently Tallinn's coastline came into view through the September haze. The maternal city glimmered as an arrangement of Orthodox onion cupolas and Lutheran church knitting-needle spires. With a crowd of Finns I disembarked and made my way across a rain-slicked quay. The customs shed was filled with trestle tables where uniformed officials were busy opening and searching luggage. A sign announced: WELCOME TO SOVIET TALLINN, but the customs man was not too welcoming. 'How long in Tallinn do you stay?' – spoken as to an idiot. 'A week.' He looked at my passport. 'Purpose of visit?' 'Tourism,' I lied. Leaving the harbour, I walked in the direction of the Soviet high-rise Hotel Viru, where a room had been booked for me. From the restaurant on the twenty-second floor I was able to survey Tallinn at night. Through the plate-glass windows a red star fizzed over the central railway station and the toy fort-like turrets of the medieval castles described by Kross in *Four Monologues on St George.*

Kross did not come to prominence in the English-speaking world until 1992, when his fifth novel *The Czar's Madman* appeared in translation. Unquestionably this is his masterpiece; narrated through a mosaic of journals, diary entries, memoranda and other writings, the novel has the grand sweep and pleasurable density of Tolstoy. 'Kross is a great writer in the old, grand style,' Doris Lessing wrote in the *Spectator* in 2003. The novel concerns the alleged insanity of a Baltic-German aristocrat, Timotheus von Bock, who was stationed in 1820s Livonia (present-day Estonia and Latvia) in the period just after *War and Peace.* Baron von Bock has the temerity to send Tsar Alexander I a dangerously frank list of proposals for constitutional reform and upbraids him for his maltreatment of serfs. For this reckless and solitary act of rebellion the Baron is imprisoned for nine years in the fortress of Schlüsselburg east of St Petersburg, and then released into house arrest on his estate at Voisiku in present-day Estonia. Coincidentally or not, Kross had served almost the same term in the Gulag. For eight years between 1946 and 1954 he slaved in a coalmine near the feared Vorkuta camp west of the Urals and at a brickworks in the Krasnoyarsk region.

On its publication in Soviet Tallinn in 1978, *Keisri Hull* (literally, 'The Emperor's Crazy') sold an impressive 32,000 copies. Kross's paradox – is von Bock mad or does his truth-telling illuminate the 'insane' world in which he lives? – appeared to mirror the Brezhnevian psychiatric asylums and the misuse of medical diagnoses in the USSR to silence dissidents.

It opens in 1827 on von Bock's release from Schlüsselburg; all his teeth have been knocked out by janitors and he cuts a pitiful figure as he enters house arrest on his Estonian estate. A decade earlier in Estonia, his egalitarian principles had led him to educate and marry a local-born chambermaid called Eeva Mattik (she had been released from serfdom for the price of four English hounds) but he was no sooner married than, in 1818, the Tsar imprisoned him. Eeva's brother, Jakob Mattik, a teacher, has meanwhile discovered a draft of the Baron's memorandum to the Tsar and rescued from the fire a sheaf of his letters

Jaan Kross by Ellen Niit

and a boxful of official papers. Though yellowing with age, the material serves Jakob as the basis for his own meditations on Tsarist repression and the nature of the Baron's imputed 'madness'.

The Czar's Madman, a work of *Tristram Shandy*-like digressions and reflections on the nature of literary 'truth', is narrated by Jakob in the form of a journal that spans twenty-odd years up to the Baron's mysterious death (was he murdered or did he take his own life?) in 1836. Into his journal Jakob incorporates extracts from the inflammatory memorandum and seeks to reconstruct the events leading up to the Baron's arrest and incarceration. He writes partly in German. Estonians who had managed to escape serfdom could only do so if they spoke German, or Low German, a language considered at that time second only to ancient Greek. Jakob's rise from 'peasant stock' to become a man who is able to identify a Claude Lorrain engraving or a Schubert symphony was extraordinary but not without precedent in the Baltic under the Tsars. A century earlier, in 1742, a freed African slave named Abram Gannibal had been appointed Tallinn's military commander by Peter the Great's daughter Elizabeth, Empress of Russia. Gannibal happened to be the maternal great-grandfather of Alexander Pushkin. Kross had long wanted to write the story of the Cameroon-born Gannibal; but, it seems, he decided instead to chronicle that of von Bock.

The Czar's Madman is brocaded with period detail. The drawing-rooms where people read literature in one corner and play chess in another are familiar to us from Russian literature. So, too, are the many visitors to von Bock's estate who come in from the snow for glasses of tea in the long wintry nights. Jakob's affinity with Baltic nature (what he calls his 'swaying, separate world') adds to the novel's vivid immediacy of detail:

> We are surrounded by the quiet waters of the creek and the green curtain of reeds. Now and again a perch jumps, or a mallard takes off, slapping the water. The reeds rustle. Some stalks bend in curious ways. As you get closer, a single reed among millions becomes astoundingly unique: with its long narrow leaves, its dome-like top of hairy, brownish-violet spikelets, it is like a building, a flowering world of its own.

In spite of the climate of suspicion in mid-1970s Moscow, the Soviet authorities had been only too happy to help Kross research *The Czar's Madman*. It may be that von Bock (his name means 'stubborn') was viewed favourably by the Soviet censors as a social Utopian and luminary of the German Enlightenment. The real-life Timotheus von Bock had been associated with the Decembrist revolt of 1825, when young Russian aristocrats rose against the Tsarist autocracy. When *The Czar's Madman* finally appeared in Russian translation in 1985, Kross was relieved to find that it contained few distortions or deletions, despite the covert links he had made between Tsarist oppression and Soviet oppression. The novel could be read as an allegory about totalitarian communism but, equally, it could be an allegory about an absolutist nightmare anywhere. Under house arrest von Bock, a prototype prisoner of conscience, has to deal with spies and informers, some with a worse conscience than others (one invites him to write his own surveillance reports for the authorities). But he refuses to be broken by either violence or bribery.

*

My article on the Baltic under Soviet communism had scarcely appeared in the *Independent* than, in November 1988, Estonia proclaimed its sovereignty. Suddenly the entire USSR was a sandpile ready to slide. On 6 November 1991 the Russian President Boris Yeltsin (reportedly inflamed by vodka) officially terminated the USSR's existence when he banned the Communist Party within Russia. Estonia was now free and Red Tallinn had gone before I knew it.

The years passed. I sought out other books by Kross. His twelfth novel, *Professor Martens' Departure* (1984), concerns a hapless Baltic expert employed by Tsar Nicholas II to collate treatises; again it unfolds as an exercise in paradox and ambiguity. It was not until 2003 that I finally met Kross. At 83, he was frail and had recently suffered a stroke. He was living with his third wife, the poet and children's writer Ellen Niit, on the fifth floor of the Soviet-era Writers' House in Tallinn's old quarter. In him I found the modesty of the true writer, a sorrowful yet slightly mischievous presence. He said he was 'itching' to write another novel but was content for the moment to work on his memoirs. By now he had been translated into twenty-three languages; in 1992 he was given 'advance warning' that he would win the Nobel Prize for Literature and told to stay by the phone. Nadine Gordimer won that year. Kross never did.

Kross's later short stories, collected in English in 1995 under the title *The Conspiracy*, recount attempts by Estonians to flee across the Gulf of Finland to Helsinki during the Nazi occupation or their deportation to the Gulag by the Soviets. Understandably, Kross did not begin to describe his Gulag years in print until the advent of Gorbachev's perestroika in the mid-1980s. Even so, there is surprisingly little bleakness in his prison tales. Kross writes about his incarceration under dictatorship with a poignancy devoid of anger. All his work is the product of a refined and subtly ironic mind, but *The Czar's Madman* ranks with Giuseppe di Lampedusa's *The Leopard* as an historical novel of timeless importance. Jaan Kross died, at the age of 87, in Tallinn in 2007. He is one of Europe's most revered writers and I would recommend his books unreservedly.

IAN THOMSON is the author of *Primo Levi: The Elements of a Life*, and two prize-winning works of reportage, *Bonjour Blanc: A Journey through Haiti* and *The Dead Yard: Tales of Modern Jamaica*. His most recent book, *Dante's Divine Comedy: A Journey Without End*, was published in 2018.

Left, Left, Left

SELINA HASTINGS

In the early 1980s I began working on my first book, a biography of Nancy Mitford. Four of the six Mitford sisters were then still living, Pamela in the Cotswolds, Diana in Paris with her second husband Sir Oswald Mosley, Debo, wife of the Duke of Devonshire, at Chatsworth, and Jessica, always known as 'Decca', with her family in California. Throughout my research Pam, Diana and Debo were immensely kind and helpful, all of them possessed of great charm and a slightly idiosyncratic sense of humour. They invited me to stay, gave me access to hundreds of letters, and mined for my benefit lucid memories of their early lives and of their family and friends.

It was well over a year since I had begun my research when Decca came to London and agreed to see me. I was slightly apprehensive at the prospect of meeting her, aware of her somewhat confrontational reputation and her long career as a defiantly radical author and journalist. We met at the Chelsea house where she was staying, Decca grey-haired, rather stout, with a very old-fashioned upper-class voice, 'grossly affected' as one of her old friends described it. Although, unlike her sisters, I found her slightly intimidating, she answered all my questions and recalled a great deal that was invaluable about her childhood and in particular her relations with Nancy.

After the interview she asked me to walk with her down the King's Road as she had a little shopping she wanted to do. It was just before Christmas and the place was bustling. As we entered a well-known stationer Decca immediately instructed me to distract the assistant standing behind the counter. As I did so I saw her out of the corner of my eye quietly sliding sheets of wrapping-paper into her handbag.

It must have been over a year later when we met again, Decca this time accompanied by her second husband, the campaigning left-wing lawyer Robert Treuhaft. I remember taking them both to a small restaurant near where I lived. It was at the time of the Falklands War, and during dinner Decca railed against the appalling behaviour of the British in launching such a brutal and unwarranted attack on the Argentinian Malvinas. Suddenly, by now far from sober, she pushed her chair back, clambered on to it, and began furiously berating our fellow diners, all of whom, to my immense relief, politely returned, after a moment of shock, to conversation with their companions and eating their dinners. Bob Treuhaft, for his part, sat amiably unconcerned, as if this were the kind of performance he had witnessed many times before.

The roots of such insurrection had been firmly planted during Decca's early years, a period described with remarkable humour and perception in *Hons and Rebels* (1960). Born in 1917, Decca was the sixth of seven siblings who grew up at Swinbrook, a small village in the Cotswolds; here her father, Lord Redesdale, had built a large square house described by Decca as something between a lunatic asylum and a barracks. Of the seven children six were girls, the eldest, Nancy, born in 1904, the youngest, Deborah, always known as Debo, in 1920. Their brother Tom, his parents' favourite, was away most of the time at school, and was later killed while fighting in Burma during the war. In childhood Decca was closest to the sisters nearest to her in age, Unity and Debo, with both of whom she racketed about, teasing and tormenting their elders. With Debo, who had a passion for the chickens her mother kept, Decca

Decca, aged 4

formed a society of two, known as The Hons (the 'H' pronounced as in 'hen'), their aim being to provoke as much family mayhem as possible.

Decca's relationship with her parents, always addressed as 'Muv' and 'Farve', was somewhat distant, her mother kind but emotionally detached, her father deeply eccentric, frequently exploding into terrifying rages. Both were staunch supporters of the Conservative Party, Muv canvassing for the Tories at elections, Farve attending Parliament to vote against such outrageous motions as allowing the entry of women into the House of Lords.

By her early teens Decca's closest bond was with Unity, whose bizarre misbehaviour she much admired, despite their rigorously opposing views. The two of them shared a sitting-room, Unity's territory scattered with fascist insignia, Decca's exhibiting a hammer-and-sickle flag and a small bust of Lenin. Both relentlessly rebelled against the series of governesses employed to teach them, none of whom stayed for more than a few weeks. As the years passed, Decca felt increasingly trapped, 'caught in a time-proofed corner of the world . . . [while] the months and years dragged slowly by, like the watched pot that never boils'.

By the time of her first London season in 1935, Decca was smouldering: she hated the world into which she had been born and now longed to leave. A committed socialist, her mind was firmly focused on running away, and an irresistible opportunity presented itself the following year with the outbreak of the Spanish Civil War. The war profoundly divided the Mitfords, Unity and Diana passionately pro-Franco, while Decca immediately became a committed Loyalist, determined somehow to leave England and join the fight in Spain. 'Fortress aspects of life at home now came to the forefront with a vengeance,' she recalled. 'I was in headlong opposition to everything the family stood for.'

It was during this period that Decca met a young man who had himself been fighting for the Loyalists, now invalided home at the age of only 19. Esmond Romilly, a cousin of the Mitfords and nephew of Winston Churchill, had rebelled from an early age against the world into which he had been born. At 15, he had run away from school, shortly afterwards launching an anti-fascist magazine, *Out of Bounds*, which had immediately impressed Decca when she came across it. Esmond was ruthless and determined, with a 'violent and rollicking personality', as one of his friends, Philip Toynbee, described him. A left-wing extremist, although never a member of the Communist Party, Esmond despised his peers and loved to cause trouble. He was a born anarchist, Toynbee recalled, 'belligerent, bullying, brave . . . the least introspective person I have ever known . . . his only conscious interest was in action'.

Decca met Esmond at a house-party and was immediately smitten. The two of them quickly bonded, within hours making secret plans to escape and join the war in Spain. This they achieved, Decca having tricked her parents into believing she had been invited to stay with family friends in France. Locked into a 'conspiracy of two against the world', the pair of them made their way to Bilbao, where Esmond found work typing dispatches for an English newspaper. Inevitably the couple were soon discovered and eventually escorted on board a Royal Navy destroyer en route to St Jean de Luz. Here, after a bitterly acrimonious battle with both their families, they were finally allowed to marry, in a brief ceremony on 18 May 1937, at the British consulate in Bayonne. Shortly afterwards the young Romillys returned to London, where they moved into a small house overlooking the docks at Rotherhithe.

With little money, they managed to survive for a while, Esmond for a brief period working as a stocking salesman. Both quickly became adept at dodging payment of bills and at stealing from the grand country houses to which they occasionally managed to wangle an invitation to stay. Decca soon became pregnant but lost her baby after only a few months. It was a devastating experience, fortifying the couple's decision to leave for America, Esmond determined to

Esmond and Decca running their bar in Miami

avoid conscription and an imminent war of which he passionately disapproved.

Arrived in New York, the Romillys were quickly taken up by a number of left-leaning and wealthy Americans, who entertained them lavishly and at length in Manhattan, Westchester County and Martha's Vineyard. Eventually they ended up in Florida, with Esmond, assisted by Decca, working as a barman in Miami, in Decca's words, 'the most unattractive town I had ever seen'. It was while in Miami, and after the German invasion of France in 1940, that Esmond's attitude towards the war suddenly changed; he flew to Toronto to enlist in the Canadian Royal Air Force, while Decca, now with a small baby, remained behind, staying with friends in Washington.

This is where *Hons and Rebels* ends. Decca reveals nothing about the subsequent weeks and months, about joining her husband in Toronto, his transfer to England in August 1941, or his death only three months later, shot down during a bombing raid over Hamburg. It was not until nearly twenty years later that her remarkable memoir was published, by which time she had long been settled in California, had remarried and become the mother of two more children, as well as a famously fanatical crusader against right-wing movements and what she regarded as the corruption and injustices of the American way of life.

Relations with her English family remained complex – relatively peaceful over the years with Nancy, Debo and Pam, unrelentingly hostile towards Unity, who died in 1948, and towards Diana, whose fascist sympathies she was unable to forgive. After the success of *Hons and Rebels*, Decca wrote several more books, including *The American Way of Death*, an investigation into the deceptions and dishonesty of the funeral industry. But it is *Hons and Rebels* for which she rightly remains best known, a remarkable portrait of an eccentric family depicted by one of its most eccentric members.

SELINA HASTINGS worked for fourteen years on the books page of the *Daily Telegraph*, then as literary editor of *Harper's & Queen*. She has written six biographies, the first a life of Nancy Mitford (1985), her most recent of Sybille Bedford (2020).

Jessica Mitford's *Hons and Rebels* (320pp) is now available in a limited and numbered cloth-bound edition of 2,000 copies (subscribers: UK & Eire £17, Overseas £19; non-subscribers: UK & Eire £18.50, Overseas £20.50).

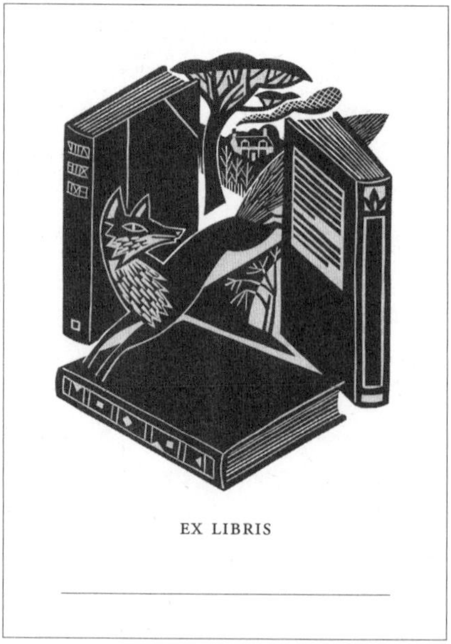

The new *Slightly Foxed* bookplate, available in packs of 100. To order please ring the office or visit our website.

An Obscure Form of Magic

EDMUND GORDON

I've just read *Party Going* (1939), Henry Green's comic and melancholic masterpiece, for the third or fourth time, and I'm still not sure how to convey its complex flavour. It's a fantastically busy and exuberant novel, in which nothing really happens. (The major events include: an old lady picking up a dead pigeon and subsequently feeling ill; a beautiful young woman having a bath; a servant getting a kiss from a stranger.) It's at once so beautifully written that I want to quote the whole thing, and so eccentrically stylized that it isn't easy to find a quotable line. (Green was intolerant of standard English grammar and syntax; witness for example his take-'em-or-leave-'em approach to articles, as in the novel's bizarre opening sentence: 'Fog was so dense, bird that had been disturbed went flat into a balustrade and slowly fell, dead, at her feet.') It's an effervescent comedy of manners, set almost exclusively among members of the English upper class – and yet its most remarkable quality is an anguished sense of human suffering.

The set-up is straightforward enough. A group of empty-headed young socialites – the sort of people you might encounter in a novel by Nancy Mitford or Evelyn Waugh – are stranded in a London railway station when thick fog delays the train taking them on holiday to France. Made uncomfortable by the growing crowd, they seek refuge in the station hotel, where they pass the time by flirting, gossiping, drinking too much, keeping secrets from one another, and

---

Henry Green, *Party Going* (1939)
New York Review of Books · Pb · 192pp · £14 · ISBN 9781681370705

trying to make each other jealous. Max Adey, the party's excessively rich and handsome host, reckons his time would be most rewardingly spent in seducing one of his guests, the highly strung Miss Julia Wray. Perhaps that's why he hasn't invited his on-off girlfriend Amabel, a famous beauty, but his plans are complicated when she turns up anyway. The trysts and tiffs between these three form the most substantial of the novel's many tangled threads, but the other members of the party are all given their own moments in the spotlight too.

Green observes them with an almost anthropological eye. One character has 'an expression so bland, so magnificently untouched and calm she might never have been more than amused and as though nothing had ever been more than tiresome'. Two young women compliment each other's clothes, 'but it was as though two old men were swapping jokes, they did not listen to each other they were so anxious to explain'. We're left in little doubt that Green himself stands firmly on the side of the servants – left outside the hotel to guard their employers' luggage against the crowd – and of the taxi driver whom one of the party fails to pay. But his intentions go much deeper than mere social criticism, and his empathy extends even to the silliest of his well-heeled protagonists.

Through some obscure form of magic, Green manages to present his characters as simultaneously ridiculous and poignant, revealing their most inane pretensions to be the products of their deepest fears. They care so much about money because they sense that it's the only thing that distinguishes them from the crowd, and also from one another; they talk so much guff about trivial subjects because they're terrified of silence. None of them seems to understand either themselves or one another very well, and it's one of Green's most cunning tactics that he often gives the impression of not understanding them very well himself. The result, as I'm not the first to point out, is that the reader feels almost protective of them – as if we know them better even than their creator does.

Henry Yorke, who wrote under the pen name of Henry Green

In a talk for BBC radio, broadcast in 1950, Green expressed reservations about conventional techniques for depicting character, from authorial summary to interior monologue:

> Do we know, in life, what other people are really like? I very much doubt it. We certainly do not know what other people are thinking and feeling. How then can the novelist be so sure?

These aren't questions that seem to trouble most novelists – or indeed most readers of novels. Showing a character in the round and even peeping inside their heads: without such contrivances, modern fiction would scarcely exist. Green's misgivings set him apart from Joyce and Proust – two of the writers he most admired – and place him in the company of Beckett and the *nouveau roman*. Except that, unlike Beckett, Green was actually interested in people. He was committed to observing the deep mystery of human beings, and to rendering social interactions in all their muddle and ambiguity. It's this mixture of avant-garde aesthetics and emotional realism that makes his novels unlike any others I know. The characters in *Party Going* have a strange lack of substance – they flicker in and out of focus – but such is the force of their agitation and uncertainty that they become somehow more vivid, more real, than the solid, scrutable creations of more conventional writers. Here is Julia, reflecting on Max's claim that he was delayed getting to the station because he had to meet his lawyer:

> Julia knew he was a liar, it was one of those things one had to put up with when one was with him. But it did seem to her unfair that he should go and spoil it all now that he was here. She had forgotten how much she resented his not turning up in her pleasure at seeing him, and now he was telling them this fairy tale about his lawyer. People were cruel. But perhaps he had wanted to make his will. Anything might happen to any one of them, everything was so going wrong. As she looked about her, at the other travellers, she could get no comfort out of what she saw. Perhaps he was not lying, which was frightening enough, but if he was then why was he lying?

In just a few lines, Julia goes from knowing that Max is lying, to doubting that he is, to doubting her very safety – 'anything might happen to any one of them' – and this vertiginous descent into confusion and fear isn't prompted by anything external, but simply by the inexorable current of her own personality. We're able to know her, in her heightened, precarious state, the way we know people in life – that is, empirically, provisionally – rather than in the absolute way we tend to know characters in fiction. It means that Green can move us in ways that simply aren't available to most of his peers.

The fluidity of *Party Going* makes for a very unusual reading experience. Against the static backdrop of the station hotel, the shifting moods and thoughts of the characters are what carry the story along. Their dialogue meanders back and forth as they lose track of what they're saying, abandoning their own positions and taking up one another's without ever seeming to notice. Even the narrative voice trickles between different perspectives, sometimes in the course of a single sentence, or flows into a heightened register all of its own. This is something that any creative writing teacher would advise against, and it's certainly a bit disorientating at first, but it allows Green to achieve some truly magnificent effects. Towards the end of the novel, following a tentative reconciliation, Max and Amabel drift off to sleep:

> Lying in his arms, her long eyelashes down along her cheeks, her hair tumbled and waved, her hands drifted to rest like white doves drowned on peat water, he marvelled again he should ever dream of leaving her who seemed to him then his reason for living as he made himself breathe with her breathing as he always did when she was in his arms to try and be more with her.
>
> It was so luxurious he nodded, perhaps it was also what she had put on her hair, very likely it may have been her sleep reaching over him, but anyway he felt so right he slipped into it too and dropped off on those outspread wings into her sleep with his, like two soft evenings meeting.

Max's intimation of bliss with Amabel doesn't last long – as soon as he wakes, five minutes later, he starts thinking of Julia again – but in the intensity with which he communicates such gusts of feeling, Green more than justifies the idiosyncrasies of his technique. Perhaps the greatest paradox of *Party Going* is that such a mannered, arty, frankly experimental book – one that places such sustained emphasis on the vagueness and shallowness of its characters – should in the end seem so natural, so rich, and so astonishingly intimate.

EDMUND GORDON won the 2017 *Slightly Foxed* Best First Biography Prize for *The Invention of Angela Carter.*

Giving Pain a Voice

ROSE BARING

A lone doctor hares down a country lane in his Land Rover, his thumb jammed on the horn to warn the oncoming traffic that he's not stopping. A woodman's been pinned to the ground on a remote hillside by a falling tree and every second counts. Even at the start of *A Fortunate Man: The Story of a Country Doctor* (1967), we are given an inkling of what makes Dr Sassall an exceptional GP. He had his thumb on the horn partly, he explains, so that the man under the tree might hear it and know he is on his way. Dr Sassall understands that even when the immediate danger is physical, his patients need him to keep their minds in mind. A good doctor treats the whole of his patient, not just his wounds.

We're in Gloucestershire, in the Forest of Dean in the 1960s, and John Berger has spent three months shadowing his remarkable friend the local GP night and day, to paint a portrait of his life. He has also recruited the Swiss documentary photographer Jean Mohr to take photographs to accompany the text. The grainy black-and-white images start by capturing the landscape against which the human drama is set, or behind which it hides. As the book progresses, they focus in – the doctor in his tweed jacket, with tie and pipe, or shirt sleeves rolled up to perform some minor surgery; his patients, sometimes looking him in the eye and hanging on his words, sometimes sitting alongside him as they spill their woes. And the community – debating, dancing, drinking.

John Berger, *A Fortunate Man: The Story of a Country Doctor* (1967)
Canongate · Pb · 176pp · £9.99 · ISBN 9781782115038

Berger sets the scene with six vignettes. This is an impoverished area of rural England, where few people own passports and not all have ventured as far as London. 'The windows were overgrown with thick ivy and since there was no plaster ceiling and holes in the rafters, the room scarcely seemed geometric and was more like a hide in a wood.' It's *Cider with Rosie* country a generation or so later. There's an isolated feel to the people – their cottages are miles along a single track or high on a lonely hill. Education is often elementary, families look after their own and society is stratified, with working people cowed and taken advantage of by their superiors. We see the doctor using his middle-class authority to intercede on their behalf, whether with the local job centre or the housing authorities. Without his voice, no one would listen to these ordinary country folk, and Dr Sassall recognizes this as part of his wide-ranging responsibilities.

In some ways it's very much a book of its time. Part of its intense appeal to me, born in 1961, are the aspects of my childhood it brings back to life. Like Dr Sassall, the Dr Skeggs and Dr Brill of my early years were never to be seen without a tweed jacket and tie and spent a good part of their day on home visits. Just when all else was topsy-turvy – loo seat too cold to sit on, day and night blurred into one, and plots from my bedside bookshelves bleeding into one another in my fevered dreams – one of them would arrive with reassuring authority to tame the illness by giving it a name and issuing an illegible prescription. I remember craning my neck to see what else those brown leather doctors' bags contained besides a thermometer, an otoscope and a freezing stethoscope, but I don't remember anything more complicated than a lollipop stick to hold my tongue down. And on some occasions, though for what reason I'm still unclear, they would produce one of those hammers which hilariously caused your leg to shoot up in the air if applied to the right spot. Did they do that just to make us laugh, as part of the treatment?

Along with the nostalgia for a time when home visits were the norm and you could get an appointment with your own doctor on

Photograph by Jean Mohr

the same day, reading *A Fortunate Man* also reminded me of the suffocating restrictiveness of that respectful and respectable world. Like my doctors, Dr Sassall provided a cradle-to-grave service, and it was often by knowing the whole family, or the extended community, that he came to figure out what was going on. Only when chatting with some women in a house where he was delivering a baby, for example, did he discover years later the cause of one patient's irresolvable psychosomatic problems. She had been seduced by her manager at the local dairy. He had promised marriage and then abandoned her, but the young woman could not bring herself to mention the pain he caused her to anyone and was fated to bear the disappointment forever in her body. Today she might have felt more able to open up.

Dr Sassall considered it a failure on his part that he had not been able to elicit the cause of her distress when first she came to see him, and much of the pleasure in this meticulous, elliptical meditation on humanity and healing lies in the remarkable character of the doctor himself. Berger uses the forensic attention to detail, which made his famous *Ways of Seeing* such a success on the BBC in 1972, to capture the strengths and idiosyncrasies of his friend and bridge partner. Initially influenced by the hardy, self-contained heroes of Joseph Conrad, Dr Sassall was a driven man with a heroic sense of vocation. Self-isolating and with the highest expectations of himself, in his early years as a GP 'he imagined himself a mobile one-man hospital.

He performed appendix and hernia operations on kitchen tables. He delivered babies in caravans.'

Yet as he grew to know his patients better, he realized that they required more of him. To shoulder the responsibilities he laid on himself, he needed to pay attention to their non-medical concerns. He read Freud and, with no psychoanalyst in reach, he analysed his own character and its roots in a painful process that led to six months of sexual impotence. But when he emerged from this, he began listening to his patients on all levels, believing that 'illness is frequently a form of expression rather than a surrender to natural hazards'. In the evenings, after his supper, he offered psychotherapy to those he felt needed it. For a rural '60s GP he was way ahead of his time.

Of all the titles on my shelf of favourites, *A Fortunate Man* is the only one I stumbled upon quite by accident, when I wandered into my local bookshop in need of a break from the intensity of a workshop in which I was taking part. I've always loved the intimate and closely detailed sense of a life, a place and a time which is conjured by oral histories like Sheila Stewart's life of the farm labourer Mont Abbott, *Lifting the Latch*. *A Fortunate Man* looked as if it might offer the same. I read it in a sitting and between its covers I discovered a driven hero and a flawed man, a mirror to myself and to aspects of my own endeavours as a psychotherapist.

'He is acknowledged as a good doctor because he meets the deep but unformulated expectation of the sick for a sense of fraternity. He recognizes them.' This intimate, individual recognition of each unique human being is the bedrock of the work I try to do, and I am often surprised by how rare an experience it is. It is hard enough to offer it to my patients after eight years of training and sixteen years of my own psychotherapy. In Sassall's case, with none of that experience and no colleagues to support him, his efforts sometimes led to lengthy periods of depression.

In *A Fortunate Man*, John Berger too is involved in a profound act of recognition. By analysing Sassall's commitment to his particular patients and his profession, and by piling observation upon observation, he carefully accumulates a weight of evidence for the value of these unremarkable human lives and of those who try to care for them. By telling their stories, he brings them briefly into the light of his compassionate gaze, according dignity to their struggles as he did to those of so many other overlooked communities during his long career as a writer.

Reading Berger's afterword, written three decades after the original book, it's a shock but not a surprise to hear of Sassall's suicide. It reminded me of Dr Skeggs's long relationship with alcohol, which only surfaced after his death. The fragile balance of the 'wounded healer' is something we recognize more clearly now, but I am still surprised by how little psychological support the NHS offers its staff in their work on the cliff-edge between life and death. I wouldn't want to do my work without it.

ROSE BARING divides her weekdays between working as a psychotherapist and as a publisher. At the weekends she turns her attention to a messy vegetable patch and is determined, one day, to produce a good crop of brassicas.

A Vanished Warmth

ROBIN BLAKE

At school I loved our history lessons. I spent hours drawing plans of castles and battles, and was a binge reader of historical fiction by anyone from Rosemary Sutcliff and Henry Treece to Mary Renault and Robert Graves. A little later I enjoyed exploring first-hand evidence from the past and I particularly remember some volumes in the school library called *They Saw It Happen*. The third of these English historical anthologies, covering the years 1689–1897, was especially well-known to us because it had been compiled by bufferish Mr Charles-Edwards and suede-shoed Mr Richardson from our very own History Department.

Reading that anthology now I can see how conventional its historical pedagogy was for the 1950s. These eye-witness accounts, while entertaining and informative, read cumulatively like *1066 and All That* with a straight face. The two schoolmasters gorge themselves on accounts of British military victories, doings at court and great men, giving only token coverage to such juicy social and political issues as the railways (a Good Thing), radical politics (mobs), empire (heroic) and slavery and child labour (thoroughly Bad Things).

Humphrey Jennings's anthology of historical witness to English history, *Pandaemonium* – which existed in typescript years before the third volume of *They Saw It Happen* appeared – stretches across almost exactly the same period. Yet it is a very different proposition.

Humphrey Jennings, *Pandaemonium: The Coming of the Machine as Seen by Contemporary Observers, 1660–1886* (1985), is out of print but we can obtain second-hand copies.

Jennings has not the slightest interest in the bloody exploits of Marlborough, Anson, Nelson and Wellington, or in the intrigues of Walpole and Disraeli. He focuses instead on what was, for him, the defining driver of change in English destiny: 'the coming of the machine'.

Jennings was born in 1907, a contemporary of W. H. Auden, John Betjeman, Graham Sutherland, Michael Tippett and Carol Reed. He enjoyed a meteoric career in the 1930s, hardly straying more than two degrees of separation from the great ones of art – Stravinsky, Picasso, Breton, Magritte, Moore. By the 1930s he had worked as a literary critic, stage designer, documentary photographer and apprentice film director with the esteemed GPO Film Unit. He showed his paintings, published verse, fell in love with surrealism and even slipped for a time into the bed of Peggy Guggenheim (he was notably handsome).

In 1936 he became one of the organizers of the ground-breaking International Surrealist Exhibition at the New Burlington Galleries and a year later was one of the instigators of Mass Observation, the unprecedented sociological experiment that collected millions of pages of observations from daily life to create 'the social anthropology of our time'. All these interests fed into his crowning creative achievements, the wartime documentary shorts that included *Listen to Britain*, *Fires Were Started* and *Diary for Timothy*. They also became vital threads in the fabric of *Pandaemonium*, which by this time he had begun compiling.

The opening takes us to Hell, with Milton's thunderous vision in *Paradise Lost* of Mammon, the devil who specialized in lucre and material greed, directing gangs of devils as they 'rifl'd the bowels of their mother earth' to grub out gold and other precious minerals. These are the raw materials to build Pandaemonium, the capital city of Hell, a colossal monument to wealth, luxury and material vanity. This brilliant opening quotation is followed by Jennings's note that the building of Pandaemonium 'began *c.* 1660. It will never be finished . . . [It] is the real history of Britain for the last three hundred years.'

Jennings, with the practising surrealist's eye for the unusual, and the film-maker's delight in intercutting and creative collage, goes on to illustrate how science and technology, once stirred into life around the time of Milton's epic, began a rolling snowball's progress that would crush and scatter the remnants of old thinking, and recreate the world in a vast new materialist vein. Jennings's purpose was to convey the magnificence of it all but also, like Milton extolling the splendours of the satanic city, not to let you forget that this is Hell. The terrible cost of the Industrial Revolution, in ecological damage and human suffering, is never far from his thoughts. There is never an out-season for these matters, but few readers of *Pandaemonium* will miss their pertinence right now.

The story is told in a succession of literary 'images' in chronological order and divided into four parts. The first covers the new realism with which writers and intellectuals began to think about Nature and society, as exemplified by one 1660 report to the Royal Society, in a house-style which Jennings glosses as 'a cold, inch-by-inch analysis and reportage of the effects of a thunderstorm, equally without reference to God or man'.

In Jennings's second section, titled 'Exploitation, 1730–1790', we read how this new thinking played out in economic terms. There is open-cast and then deep mining, there are scorching ironworks and the first factories and workhouses. This period produced Christopher Smart's madhouse poetry, a profuse outpouring of imagery dramatizing the very war of materialism against animism, which Jennings saw as a mortal settling of accounts, the death-struggle of the old order. Over it all broods the demon of land enclosure – which we would now call privatization. Great swathes of ancient common land, essential for the subsistence of the rural poor, were being systematically stolen from them, with the dual effect of further enriching the rich, and forcing great numbers of destitute men and women into either industrial work or an eighteenth-century version of the gig economy.

This realism extended to a new strain of melancholy pastoral in the arts, developed by poets such as Thomas Gray (a special interest of Jennings) and artists such as George Stubbs (a special interest of mine). Country life was no longer to be imagined as a pleasant, lazy dalliance: it was a matter of toil, overseen by dour taskmasters, and all in the interests of distant landowning plutocrats. The emotional significance of this is underscored by a passage from Oliver Goldsmith's *The Deserted Village*:

Princes or Lords may flourish or may fade;
A breath can make them, as a breath has made;
But a bold peasantry, the country's pride,
When once destroyed can never be supply'd.

These developments may have been deplored by many in the eighteenth century, but they were rarely seen as resistible. Then a new note is struck: Revolution. Part three of *Pandaemonium* shows nineteenth-century people fighting back against industrialization – as Thomas Carlyle was the first to call it – with direct action that included inchoate Luddism, agitation for parliamentary reform (as at Peterloo) and Chartism. Eloquent support for these causes came from writers of all sorts.

Shelley's 372-line poem 'The Mask of Anarchy', written in white-hot anger at the massacre at Peterloo, and Byron's sardonic maiden speech in the House of Lords against the bill to make the breaking of machines a capital offence, are two outstanding moments. Others are the German observer Friedrich Engels's mistakenly optimistic observation of South Lancashire industrially transformed into a perfect seedbed for a new proletarian consciousness; Henry Mayhew's unique first-hand reports on the lives of the poor; the sanctimonious purblindness of Charles Kingsley ('Those who live in towns should carefully remember this . . . *Never lose an opportunity of seeing something beautiful.* Beauty is God's handwriting'); and Thomas Carlyle's prophecies ringing with doom – 'England is dying of inanition.'

In a vivid, barbed description of his visit to the ideal factory-town of Robert Owen in 1819, Robert Southey writes that Owen's 'humour, his vanity, his kindliness of nature lead him to make these *human machines* as he calls them (and literally believes them to be) as happy as he can . . . And he jumps at once to the monstrous conclusion that, because he can do this with 2,210 persons who are totally dependent on him, all mankind might be governed with the same facility.'

William Blake's is the most remarkable of all these revolutionary voices. If the poem denouncing 'dark satanic mills' could hardly have been left out, there are other less familiar Blakean passages here, including a monetized parody of the Lord's Prayer: 'Give us day by day our Real Taxed Substantial Money bought Bread; deliver from the Holy Ghost whatever cannot be taxed; for all is debt between Caesar and us and one another; lead us not to read the Bible but let our Bible be Virgil and Shakespeare; and deliver us from Poverty in Jesus, that Evil One.'

The final section of *Pandaemonium* is titled 'Confusion', and begins in 1851. Superficially the confusion is not very apparent. The *Pax Victoriana* has arrived in all its pomp, railways crisscross the land, whole reaches of the country are given over to factories, the Great Exhibition has opened in the Crystal Palace, and social complacency has set in as firmly as one of Mrs Beeton's pink blancmanges. The mob, the recurrent cause of societal chaos, has been tamed, and now, in between betting on dogs and racing pigeons, it trots along to the Crystal Palace at a shilling a time to marvel at the wonders of mechanized industry.

But for intellectuals there is sickness in the heart of the iron roses that decorate Paxton's gigantic greenhouse. It is becoming increasingly difficult to square material progress with what has been irreparably lost. John Ruskin glooms over the railway's destruction of landscape and wonder ('And now the valley is gone, and the Gods with it, and now every fool in Buxton can be at Bakewell in half an hour'), and two distinctive heirs of Blake, the naturalist Richard Jefferies and the socialist and campaigner for many progressive causes,

Confusion, on Ludgate Hill

Edward Carpenter, find life terminally impoverished under, as Carpenter has it, 'the falsehood of a gorged and satiated society'. Even Charles Darwin rues, and cannot quite account for, the loss of his youthful love of poetry, especially Shakespeare, who now 'nauseates me'. 'My mind', he writes in 1881, 'seems to have become a kind of machine for grinding general laws out of large collections of facts' and adds that 'the loss of these tastes is a loss of happiness'.

Jennings's closing passage underlines this sense of loss by quoting the last page of William Morris's *A Dream of John Ball*. In this novella Morris dreams of meeting John Ball and other heroes of the fourteenth-century Peasants' Revolt, and absorbs Ball's mantra that 'fellowship is life and lack of fellowship is death'. Jennings got from Morris the idea that the machine interferes with human fellowship and, in one of the notes that pepper *Pandaemonium*'s text, he argues that this is the origin of the Victorian era's regrettable addiction to sentimentality. 'Banish human comradeship from life and the naked psyche looks longingly round for an image with which to identify. An image of death and tears and despair: withered grapes, funeral palls or modern machine images, which it can make symbolic of vanished warmth.'

Although there are hopeful passages in this fourth section of the book, Morris's awakening from his dream is more characteristic of its mood. Jennings might have ended on an up-note by highlighting the quasi-socialist discourse between Morris and Ball, or even with an extract from Morris's hopeful essay 'The Factory as It Might Be'. Instead we see the dreamer awakened by dawn 'hooters' summoning the factory hands to begin another day at the devil's work.

Humphrey Jennings never saw *Pandaemonium* in print. He was still collecting material and writing notes for the project in 1950 when, at the age of 43, he fell from a rock while researching a film in Greece, and died from the resulting head injury. The book was assembled and published thirty-five years later by Jennings's old Mass Observation colleague Charles Madge and his daughter Mary-Lou Jennings. She writes in a preface that her father would quote the French writer Apollinaire's insistence on the kinship between poetry and history: that only in the past can poets learn imaginatively who they are and what they might become. While some of the 'images' in Jennings's book are indeed fine poetry, most are prose passages. But the final effect is that of a great poetic construction, a *tour de force* of the imagination. Jennings's chosen writers do not so much 'see it happen' as feel it in their bones.

ROBIN BLAKE's sixth mystery novel about eighteenth-century Preston, *Death and the Chevalier*, was published in 2019.

Loafing by the Seine

KRISTIAN DOYLE

Sometimes, nostalgic for Paris, I read books about the city in the hope that through them I'll know again the felt reality of daily life there. It never really works: books, after all, can only do so much. A rare few, though, come surprisingly close. Among them *Paris*, by Julian Green, first published in French in 1983, is the one I return to most often. It is also, for some reason, one of the least known.

I have no memory of how I first came to it (it seems now to be one of those near-mythical objects that appear out of nowhere at just the right moment). But I do remember very clearly reading its perfect opening sentence and believing, only a few lines in, that I was holding something I could trust. 'I have often dreamed of writing a book about Paris', it begins, 'that would be like one of those long, aimless strolls on which you find none of the things you are looking for but many that you were not looking for.'

That Green managed to realize this dream seems to his readers, holding the published, highly (if not widely) praised book, only natural – but it was likely a surprise to him. Its composition turned out to be very different from what he'd anticipated. Rather than being a seamless and unified whole that was written straight through and then published, *Paris* was cobbled together near the end of his long life from wildly various, and occasionally contradictory, essay-like first-person bits and pieces that he'd written over many decades. Some were from so long ago that he must hardly have recognized

---

Julian Green, *Paris* (1983)
Penguin · Pb · 144pp · £8.99 · ISBN 9780141194653

them. That opening line, for example, is from a section written in 1945, almost forty years before the book itself was published.

Then again, forty years might not seem much to a writer whose career was almost twice as long. Green, born in Paris in 1900, was known mainly for writing one of the most substantial diaries in French letters – nineteen volumes, covering the years 1919 to 1998. He also wrote a great deal of fiction – much of it also long, and long-winded – over the same period, his first novel, *Mont-Cinère*, being published in 1926, and his last, *Dixie*, in 1994.

Paris, though it might well end up being the one book of his to endure in the English-speaking world, is an anomaly in his body of work. He was, almost by profession, a prose maximalist. And yet *Paris* is the short, scrappy notebook of a born poet, someone inspired in fits and starts, too close to his impressions, and ignorant of the architectural requirements of a long work of prose. A glance at the chapter titles, which range freely between the particular and the general, the concrete and the poetic (e.g. 'Val-de-Grâce church', 'Museums, streets, seasons, faces', 'Lost cries'), and at the endnotes, which show the seemingly random ordering of those chapters, gives you an idea of the book's lack of pattern.

It's also somewhat of an anomaly when it comes to the great Paris books. There are few references to the city's well-known architectural glories ('I shall be making no mention of the great monuments or any of the places you would expect to find duly described'), it doesn't go in search of the down-and-out or the demi-monde, there's no carnality or clichéd City-of-Light *amour*, and there are none of the mysterious objectivized women the surrealists – his contemporaries – were so obsessed with: in fact, there are hardly any people in it at all. You often hear cities in books described as being themselves characters – here Paris is, aside from its author, really the *only* character.

Green's work does have one important thing in common with many of the great Paris books of his own era, though: it takes place not in some objective, strictly exact Paris, but in a Paris that is as much a projection of the author's psyche as a reflection of reality. It is a dream-book, a collection of visions:

> During the long war years, when I was living far from Paris, I used to wonder how so large a city found room inside a tiny compartment of the human brain. Paris, for me, had become a kind of inner world through which I roamed in those difficult dawn hours when despair lies in wait for the waking sleeper . . . Thinking about [it] all the time, I rebuilt it inside myself. I replaced its physical presence with something else, something almost supernatural . . . As time went on, this transposed Paris was in danger of becoming a little more abstract each day. I could see it all right, I used to look at it all the time, but . . . it was a Paris of visions in which I took my walks now, a Paris that, though intensely real, was imperceptibly migrating from flesh to spirit.

This is the book's heart: everything in it comes from these self-aware declarations. That such a deeply personal Paris can also be ours is down to the fineness of his perception and the communicatory power of his language. He never forgets that his antecedents are, as he says, the 'novelists and poets' – Proust and Baudelaire in particular – 'whose job it is to see as if for the first time'. The evidence is there on every page, even in off-hand descriptions. 'This evening a light mist covered Paris, and the chestnut trees, lit from within by the streetlamps, were like huge Japanese lanterns'; 'An endless sunbeam slices the church in two, passing between the columns as between sequoias in an American forest'; 'Marvellous gardens whose bluish distances, as in a painting, ran down to the banks of the Seine'; 'Notre-Dame . . . its depths, its echoes, and all the night-time it harbours within its walls'.

For Green, though, descriptions of the tangible world, however perfect they might be, are not enough. Near the end of the book he considers certain paintings of Paris that, though skilful, fall short of a true representation of the city. 'While all the trees are in the right places and the houses are depicted with scrupulous accuracy,' he writes, 'something is missing, and that something is Paris itself, the invisible presence of Paris, the spirit that informs the light and shade of foliage on the stones.' Capturing this spirit – which, despite the myriad ways in which Paris has changed in the decades since those words were written, still exists – is Green's ultimate goal. Somehow, in fewer than a hundred pages, he achieves it.

Though it takes for its ostensible subject one of the loftiest cities in human history, it is nevertheless a profoundly intimate book. But it's not an intimacy achieved by opening up to, or even addressing directly, the reader: mostly Green seems to be speaking only to himself, as he tries, sometimes desperately, to give form to feeling, to capture the beloved city of his memory and daily experience in his own mind. It's as if he's letting us overhear him talking to himself.

Most of the sections read as though they were written with little thought of publication. They are full of the strange tonal shifts and apparently beside-the-point reveries typical of an interior monologue. 'I made the discovery that Paris is shaped like a human brain,' begins one typical example.

> [It] tickled my fancy to suppose I had been born in the realm of imagination and had grown up in the domain of memory . . . sometimes it seemed right to me that the capital should recall its history through the medium of the Marais, perform its intellectual tasks with the aid of the fifth district, and do its sums in the Stock Exchange quarter; running through it all, however, there was the River Seine, which to my mind represented the instinctive, unspoken part of our nature, like a great current of vague inspirations blindly seeking an ocean in which to drown themselves . . .

For all the intimacy of his voice, though, he remains an endlessly elusive figure, as mysterious as his city. On the rare occasions when he does reveal himself, it's in his daydreams, almost accidentally. Take for instance his reverie about the city's staircases. 'How absorbed people look as they climb from floor to floor', he writes.

> So many resolutions reached, so many anxious questions to which the answers lie in wait behind the door that is about to open! Here on the stairs is the time and the place before making up your mind, that final moment of reflection . . . As a result there appears to linger, in some of those great circular stairwells, a memory . . . of the meditations in which love, lust, and world-weariness fought for the hearts of all the nameless people who ever passed that way.

This is a typical Green passage, haunted with longing, beautiful and true despite its theatricality, its burden of abstractions. But then, carried away, he goes on, into something rarer:

> But if these interior staircases tease one's curiosity, what soothing melancholy is poured into the stroller's heart by the flights of stone steps inviting him down to the Seine to loaf there, lost in contemplation of its dark waters! It is a good place, the lower embankment, to take your dreams for a walk . . . [It] exerts a secret hold on the kind of man who is given to roving meditations and whose heart feeds on regrets. As he climbs back up the steps, it is with the feeling that he has laid in a store of memories and is richer by a fresh sadness.

Nowhere else does he come as close to self-portraiture. Here – in the figure of the anonymous insatiably nostalgic stroller, loafing by the Seine, at ease with solitude and immersed in the dark give-and-take of his own remembering – he stands revealed, if only for an instant.

KRISTIAN DOYLE is a writer based in Liverpool. He is currently at work on a novel.

Charles Keeping

The Last of Rome

SUE GAISFORD

Desperation drove me to Horatius, one gloomy afternoon in late October. Thirty restless children were waiting to be entertained, educated or even just dissuaded from rioting by their hapless supply teacher. I gave them Macaulay's *Lays of Ancient Rome* – largely because my father's recitation of 'How Horatius Kept the Bridge' had so grabbed and held my own attention, decades earlier. The drama of the thing still worked its magic: the bridge fell with a crash like thunder, whereupon 'a long shout of triumph rose from the walls of Rome / As to the highest turret-tops was splashed the yellow foam'. My father would put gleeful stress on the word 'yellow'. Then, of course, brave Horatius, fully armed and uttering a powerful prayer to Father Tiber, hurls himself into the turbulent river and makes it to the other shore.

It was but a short step to the writings of Rosemary Sutcliff. For a bookish child, discovering more about the ancient world in which she was so at home was unadulterated pleasure. Her Romans became more immediate, fallible, brave, attractive and alarming than anyone I ever encountered in outer Surrey. Reading her, history came brilliantly and noisily to life, and was to remain a lasting passion for all of us who came under her spell, which I'd bet includes half the life-members of the National Trust.

You could also bet that she knew her Macaulay. Towards the end of *Frontier Wolf*, young Alexios, now wearing the emerald dolphin ring of the Aquila family, is leading his weary and wounded troops at speed, away from their indefensible fort on the Firth of Forth. They are a mixed bag, few with more than a tenuous connection to Rome, but they have developed a personal loyalty to Alexios, and are on his side. To have any chance of escaping their pursuers, they must destroy the bridge on the road to Bremenium. The men work furiously with axes, crowbars and ropes, some waist-deep in icy water, leaving only a few to stand and fight off the vengeful tribal armies until, when it seems almost impossible, 'there was a whining and cracking of timbers, and, with a rending crash the whole thing keeled over, and its centre and near end swept downriver in a tossing welter of beams and planking'.

But Lucius, a learned, avuncular officer whom we have come to love, is mortally wounded. Immediately, the focus narrows until we are alone with him, and Alexios comforting him:

> 'You've had a hard morning's work. Go to sleep now.'
>
> And like a tired child, he turned his head on Alexios's knee and settled his cheek. He gave a small, dry cough, and that was all.
>
> It was like Lucius, his Commanding Officer thought, to die so quietly and neatly.

It takes a great writer to zoom in from the furious heat and clangour of battle to such a tender moment and then, heaving a deep sigh, to send the tattered remnants of an exhausted army further south, into the leaden dawn, towards the safety of the Wall.

It is the year 343, and the effete Emperor Constans, visiting Britain, offers Alexios another command, well away from the inhospitable north. He spends a moment looking back on it all, on 'the hills of his lost wilderness' where many previously strong Roman forts now lie abandoned, where he had grown to maturity, and where he knows that he will never walk again.

In *The Lantern Bearers*, set a century later, it is the old, blind Flavian, a descendant of Alexios, who now wears the dolphin ring. His son Aquila, like his ancestors, marches with the legions, but as soon as he arrives home on leave he is ordered back to port, for by now the Romans are finally abandoning Britain. In a moment of crisis he decides that, despite deeply divided loyalties, his place is with his family, rooted through generations in their old farm in the gentle South Downs. He deserts from the army – just in time to see the farm razed to the ground, his father killed and his sister carried off by Saxon Sea-Wolves. As the Dark Ages close in, Aquila gradually learns that he must become one of the lantern bearers: the physician Eugenus explains that it is 'for us to keep something burning, to carry what light we can forward into the darkness and the wind'.

Aquila's adventures take him into slavery in Viking galleys, land him on the northern shores of Scandinavia and eventually bring him back to Kent, to Tanatus or the Isle of Thanet, the 'great burg of Hengist', where he manages to regain his freedom and eventually to become a married man, a father, an uncle and, once again, a soldier, though by now Rome is long gone and he is fighting for the Britons.

His own fateful bridge is across the Medway at Durobrivae, now Rochester. This time he is himself one of the little band defending it against Hengist's ferocious advance-guard, those blue-eyed snarling Saxons who had burned his home and killed his father. And it is he who, like Horatius, springs with a shout of triumph into the 'immensity of nothingness opening behind him . . . and the cold water . . . engulfed him and closed over his head'.

These are tremendous stories, superbly written, thrilling and profound. In each novel, the central character learns to respect, value and even to love people with no blood connection with Rome – or indeed with himself. And each of them overcomes a burden of prejudice: Alexios has been condemned for abandoning a fort that could (perhaps) have been saved, while Aquila cannot conquer his hunger for revenge. Ultimately, Alexios is forced to evacuate another fort, and is this time applauded, though the major tragedy of his young life has been losing his dearest friend. And young Aquila realizes that he must finally put aside his pride and adopt the principles and

Charles Keeping

customs of the native people of Britain, for whom Rome is becoming an increasingly distant memory, as her vast, unruly empire slowly vanishes into the mists.

SUE GAISFORD is an all-purpose journalist, currently trying hard to control an obsession with Roman remains, but reluctant to plunge too deeply into the Dark Ages.

Slightly Foxed is reissuing all four of Rosemary Sutcliff's Roman novels as a set in a limited and numbered cloth-bound edition of 2,000 copies.

The third and fourth titles in the series, *Frontier Wolf* (224pp) and *The Lantern Bearers* (264pp), are now available (subscribers per copy for each title: UK & Eire £17, Overseas £19; non-subscribers: UK & Eire £18.50, Overseas £20.50). All prices include post and packing. Copies may be ordered by post (53 Hoxton Square, London N1 6PB), by phone (020 7033 0258) or via our website www.foxedquarterly.com.

The first and second books in the series, *The Eagle of the Ninth* (248pp) and *The Silver Branch* (216pp), published last year, are also still available.

Worse Things Happen at Sea

DAVID FLEMING

Every child who enjoys reading will sooner or later begin to explore the world of grown-up books. The first ones I ever read were bought in an antique shop in the picturesque town of Cromarty on the Black Isle. I can't recall my exact age or the year – about thirteen, around 1975 – but the second-hand paperbacks I found there and devoured over that three-week family holiday are very clear in my mind.

My literary hoard included a biography of Kit Carson, a POW escape story, an Arthur Hailey novel and Walter Lord's *A Night to Remember*. Of these, the only one I've returned to down the years is Lord's haunting minute-by-minute account of the sinking of the *Titanic*. Many books about this famous and ill-fated ship have come and gone, but *A Night to Remember* has outlived them all. First published in 1955, it remains in print today and is as fresh and compelling as ever.

The loss of the *Titanic* has loomed large in the popular imagination from the very beginning – thousands of people lined the quays to watch the *Carpathia* arrive in New York with the survivors. The *Titanic* was, after all, the most luxurious ship that had ever taken to the waves, boasted a passenger list which included the rich and the famous, and was popularly regarded as unsinkable – all this we know. But dull books can be written about fascinating subjects.

So why is Walter Lord's account so gripping? Put very simply, he takes us there, and he makes us care. *A Night to Remember* has no

---

Walter Lord, *A Night to Remember* (1955)
Penguin · Pb · 256pp · £9.99 · ISBN 9780141399690

routine opening chapters about the history of the White Star Line or how the ship was built. Instead, from the very start, we are there in the North Atlantic on that freezing night in 1912, high up in the crow's-nest with Frederick Fleet as he keeps lookout and suddenly sees the iceberg straight ahead. In the pages that follow we're introduced to many other characters and discover what they saw, felt and said as events unfolded over the next terrible few hours.

Lord based his narrative on interviews he had conducted with survivors of the disaster, and this gives it a directness and authenticity that no formal history could hope to match. The *Titanic* has often been considered a microcosm of Edwardian society – the rich enjoying their leisure in spacious upper staterooms, the poor cramped down below in third-class or labouring in the bowels of the ship, shovelling coal to keep the great engines turning. Lord allows us to meet them all: millionaires, stokers, stewards, ship's officers, husbands and wives, youngsters seeking a new life in America.

RMS *Titanic* in Southampton Water, 10 April 1912

A Night to Remember is the story of people caught up in extraordinary circumstances. Living in a world of terrorist atrocities and extreme weather events, it's easy for us to empathise with them as they face an unexpected and growing peril. Lord reveals how haphazard and chaotic the evacuation of passengers into the lifeboats really was. The rule of course was 'women and children first' but many wives did not want to leave their husbands, did not realize how dangerous the position was, or felt safer on the 'unsinkable ship' than adrift in a tiny open boat on the vast, cold Atlantic.

The story of who got into a lifeboat, the difference between living and dying, is central to the drama. Lord gives us many moving vignettes to illustrate this, including the self-sacrifice of some male passengers as they escorted their wives or other women to the boats: 'Mr Turrell Cavendish said nothing to Mrs Cavendish. Just a kiss . . . a long look . . . another kiss . . . and he disappeared into the crowd.' Mrs Walter D. Douglas begs her husband to come with her. '"No," Mr Douglas replied turning away, "I must be a gentleman."' Such sentiments are echoed by Benjamin Guggenheim who, along with his manservant, puts on his best clothes to go down with the ship in style.

These codes of courage and honour would soon have to rise to a more prolonged challenge in the face of the coming war's machine guns, flame-throwers and gas clouds. The failure of modern technology as personified by the *Titanic* was a prelude to its being harnessed in the cause of mass slaughter. The sinking of the *Titanic* cast a cloud over the fabled long Edwardian summer. The old certainties were beginning to fail.

Courage was not of course confined to the men. On rereading the book recently, I was struck by the story of Edith Evans who allowed another woman to climb into a boat first as she had children waiting for her at home. This caused Edith to miss her own chance as the boat was quickly lowered away. It was the last one. Anxiously looking up the passenger list provided at the end of the book, in which the survivors' names are printed in italics, my worst fears were confirmed. Miss Evans's thoughtfulness proved fatal.

Who got into a lifeboat could be frighteningly arbitrary. On the starboard side of the ship the First Officer, Murdoch, allowed men to climb in if there was room and no women were waiting; while on the other side, the Second Officer, Lightroller, played by Kenneth More in the 1958 film version, controversially forbade male passengers, including boys, any chance of escape even when the boats were half empty. Lord follows the fortunes of some men who saved themselves by jumping into boats as they were lowered, or by swimming over to them once afloat. Few who took to the ocean could survive long in such icy waters. Initiative and presence of mind saved a steerage passenger, Anna Sjoblom. Stuck down below, she managed to reach the boat deck by climbing an emergency ladder reserved for the crew.

Despite the fact that official enquiries were held on both sides of the Atlantic, an astonishing number of myths, legends and mysteries have grown up about the *Titanic* over the years, with virtually every aspect of the story being open to several interpretations. Even something as simple as whether the lookouts were supposed to have, or use, binoculars is hotly debated. Whole books have also been written on the question of the *Californian*, the ship that lay ten miles away apparently oblivious to the *Titanic*'s plight. And the actions and motivations of key figures such as Bruce Ismay, the White Star Line's Managing Director, have been put under the microscope.

Lord closes his account by noting that only a rash man would set himself up as final arbiter of all that happened. There are some aspects of the story which he doesn't tackle, such as the likely suicide of First Officer Murdoch – the man unlucky enough to have been in charge of the ship when the collision occurred. Nevertheless, for clarity and sheer readability, it is *A Night to Remember* which will continue to be the version of events that brings the sinking vividly alive and helps to immortalize all who were there.

DAVID FLEMING used to be a Customs Officer and is now a freelance writer. He lives in Broughty Ferry and enjoys looking out to sea.

Progression by Digression

CHRISTIAN TYLER

In many ways *The Life and Opinions of Tristram Shandy, Gentleman* is a maddening book. It is funny, of course, but also eccentric, anarchic and longwinded; and it's hard to understand why it survived to become a classic. Perhaps these days only university students and professors read *Tristram Shandy*. But for two centuries it was a family favourite. My great-grandfather Walter Congreve discovered it while lying wounded in hospital during the Boer War. He carried it with him – alongside the Bible – through the First World War, to his military command in Palestine and thence to Malta as governor.

Another forebear, Henrietta Maria Stanley, gave an autographed first edition of *Tristram Shandy* to her grandson Bertrand Russell when he asked for it for his birthday. Normally she was dismissive of her shy grandson: on one occasion she quizzed him about science books, none of which he had read, then turned to her roomful of visitors and sighed: 'I have no intelligent grandchildren.' But this request pleased her greatly. 'I won't write in it,' she told him, 'because people will say what an odd grandmother you have!' She inscribed it nonetheless.

One of my cousins was christened Tristram after Sterne's narrator. More recently my stepson, a former drama student, wrote a very creditable stage adaptation of the book, though it was never performed. About the same time a film appeared called *A Cock and Bull Story* (the title taken from the novel's last line) which mimicked on

---

Laurence Sterne, *The Life and Opinions of Tristram Shandy, Gentleman* (1759)
OUP · Pb · 640pp · £8.99 · ISBN 9780199532896

screen Sterne's theme of a work which is trying, but failing, to get itself written.

As for me, I suppose I owe my first job to *Tristram Shandy.* In the late '60s I was a hopeful Cambridge graduate trying to get a job on a newspaper. But jobs were scarce; and graduates were viewed (at least in the provinces) with deep suspicion. At length I was granted an interview with the *Yorkshire Post* where the editor, unimpressed, gloomily passed me on to the sister paper, the *Evening Post.*

Its editor Ewart Clay seemed more inclined to hire me. However, behind him at the interview stood the imposing figure of his deputy Edmund Hillas, who was plainly losing patience with the naïve graduate with his philosophy degree and toffy accent from the soft South. He broke in suddenly: 'Does tha' know Shandy Hall?'

There was no reason why I should. But I did. 'It's the house in Coxwold where Laurence Sterne wrote *Tristram Shandy*,' I said. Hillas was astonished. ''E knows Shandy Hall!' he exclaimed, turning to the boss. And I was in. (I thought it imprudent to add that I knew the place only because it was a few miles from my Yorkshire public school.)

One reason why the book has lasted, you could say, is that the world has finally caught up with it. For, apart from its language, *Shandy* is a postmodern novel. Ironic, self-conscious, tricksy, it breaks all the rules of structure, muddles fiction with fact, confuses author and narrator, and shamelessly displays its inner workings to the reader, who is directly addressed, cajoled and upbraided.

There are all kinds of typographical tricks: blank pages, diagrams, suggestive asterisks for the juicy bits. Chapters are out of order, pages are missing. Sterne doesn't get round to writing his preface until halfway through Volume 3. It's all part of a game to demonstrate the supposed inadequacy of language and the struggles of authorship. But Stern's facetiousness is erudite. He throws in obscure words like 'epiphonema', 'erotesis' and 'hypallage' – and he can write most elegantly when he chooses.

His models were Rabelais, Cervantes and Montaigne but his satire reminds me rather of Swift or Pope. His target seems to have been the pretensions of the Enlightenment, in particular the philosopher John Locke whose theory of the association of ideas becomes the central theme and instrument of Sterne's pseudo-academic mockery.

Digression is the dominant motif of the book. *Di*gression, says Sterne, is the art of *Pro*gression. And he uses it ruthlessly. Some of his excursions are delightful, like the story of the Abbess of Andouillets and her novice, abandoned by their carriage driver in Volume 7 and forced like muleteers to use obscenities to get the animals moving. Others are long and tedious, like the story of Slawkenbergius and noses in Volume 4. Looked at another way, this use of digression is only an exaggerated form of what was to come 150 years later. Sterne is anticipating the 'stream-of-consciousness' mode of James Joyce and Virginia Woolf. Likewise, his enjoyment of microscopic description – how Walter Shandy takes off his wig, how Corporal Trim stands while reading aloud one of parson Yorick's sermons – has been copied by many a would-be Booker winner.

When *Tristram* first appeared in 1759, some commentators were outraged that an Anglican vicar should have written a book containing so much sexual innuendo. However, women reportedly were avid readers. Sterne was no misogynist – rather the reverse – but he did have a robust attitude to sex even if it was veiled with suggestive asterisks, obscure double entendres and Latinisms which probably went over most readers' heads. Described as an irreverent but devout clergyman, Sterne I should say is bawdy rather than lewd. So we meet Dr Kunastrokius, Signor Coglionissimo and an ancient authority called Phutatorius (copulator). We learn that to 'wind up the clock' is intended as a double entendre and that 'old hats' are female genitalia ('because often felt', explains the Oxford edition). Sterne borrows copiously, but from relatively few sources: Burton's *Anatomy of Melancholy* and Chambers's *Cyclopaedia* in particular. His profligacy with names and quotations, invented and real, is an editor's nightmare; and my edition has no fewer than 54 pages of footnotes.

The central joke of *Tristram Shandy* is about Time. The narrator will never catch up with his own life. Tristram is not born until Volume 3; in the middle of Volume 4 he declares he's a year older, yet on paper he's not yet lived a whole day. The more he writes, the more he will fall behind, and so the faster he will have to write. It's good news, says Sterne, 'for papermakers and quill-pluckers'. The mature Bertrand Russell tackled the paradox in *The Principles of Mathematics*, explaining that Tristram would complete his biography, however eventful his life might be, only if he lived for ever.

Sterne's title is of course a misnomer. What we learn about Tristram amounts to little more than that his nose was damaged at birth by Dr Slop's careless application of forceps; that he was supposed to be baptised Trismegistus but the servant Susannah who carried the message couldn't pronounce the name; and that he was accidentally circumcised by a falling sash window whose cords, pulleys and counterweights had been purloined for a project on Uncle Toby's bowling green.

Which brings us to the real heart of the book: the Shandean hobby-horses. 'Shandy' is said to be Yorkshire dialect for 'crackpot'; and Uncle Toby is its chief exponent. Innocent, guileless and good-hearted, he is obsessed with military fortifications. He has been wounded at Namur, in the groin, and with the help of his loyal servant Corporal Trim spends his time recreating the sieges of the War of the Spanish Succession in his back garden. There he is watched by his 'concupiscible' neighbour the Widow Wadman whose desire for him is clouded only by anxiety about the state of his marriage-tackle.

Toby's obsession drives Walter mad; and though Walter explodes, he always forgives his tender-hearted brother. But he, too, has his hobby-horses – so many, indeed, that it's hard to find a subject on which he does *not* have an eccentric, impregnable opinion. Walter gathers opinions like fallen apples and makes them his own, says Tristram: 'His road lay so very far on one side from that wherein most men travelled.'

When he speaks of family life, the Shandys and their household staff, Sterne's humour is no longer satirical but 'sentimental' – a newly coined word meaning sympathetic and affectionate, not having our modern sense of artificial or cloying. His minor characters are important: Susannah the maid, Obadiah the 'fat, foolish scullion', Jonathan the coachman, Dr Slop and the parson Yorick (who represents Sterne himself).

Tristram Shandy was a hit with the public, and Sterne was a tireless promoter. Today he would be inviting himself to every literary festival in the country. The book's popularity waned as successive volumes emerged, while its author was meanwhile dying of 'the vile cough' tuberculosis. Volume 8 has some of the best writing of all – verbal gymnastics, monstrous metaphors and showers of synonyms. But it dribbles to a close in Volume 9 with Sterne unable to find an ending (how could such a book have one?).

Sterne aimed mainly to please. Like Sancho Panza he wanted to rule 'a kingdom of hearty laughing subjects'. True Shandeism, he declares at the end of Volume 4, 'opens the heart and lungs . . . forces the blood and other vital fluids of the body to run freely thro' its channels, and makes the wheel of life run long and chearfully [*sic*] round'. And it found many distinguished fans and imitators: Diderot, Jefferson, Nietzsche, Karl Marx and, of course, Bertrand Russell among them.

My great-grandfather (Walter, like the elder Shandy) plainly enjoyed the military nonsense. Whether you get on with *Tristram Shandy* depends, I suppose, on your sense of humour or your character, or maybe just your mood. It's best read as it suits you: skip where you want, savour where you can. Taken in small doses, it is the perfect bedside book.

On the other hand, of course, you may just find it maddening.

CHRISTIAN TYLER gratefully acknowledges Sterne's help in his career. He continues to feel sentimental towards Yorkshire.

Branching Out

HAZEL WOOD

In keeping with its name, Pimpernel Press has put down its roots in an unassuming Victorian house hidden at the end of a pleasant street off West London's Harrow Road. The only hint that a publisher is in residence is the pile of tempting-looking books glimpsed from the front doorstep through the ground-floor bay window. Pimpernel's publisher, Jo Christian, squeezes past me in the narrow hall to usher me into her combined office and living-room, where a long table is covered with a comfortable clutter of laptop, proofs, interesting objects and framed photographs. Beneath a wall thick with prints and paintings a pair of life-sized Coade stone greyhounds – refugees perhaps from some great house or garden – stand next to a large old sofa covered in piles of books. We're clearly a long way here from the world of corporate publishing.

That was the world Jo and her business partner, Gail Lynch, were escaping when they set up Pimpernel Press in 2013, following the sale to a conglomerate of the independent publisher where they both worked. During her thirty years as a commissioning editor, one of Jo's special interests had been books on gardens and gardening, and a number of her authors who fancied dealing with this new corporate world as little as she did had come to her with their projects. The decisive moment arrived when Fergus Garrett, Head Gardener at Great Dixter, the late Christopher Lloyd's famous garden, remarked that he was ready to produce the book Jo had been asking him to

---

Pimpernel Press, 22 Marylands Road, London W9 2DY. For a full list of their publications visit their website: www.pimpernelpress.com.

write for years. 'I said to Gail, what am I going to do with this?' says Jo, 'and she said, "Well, the old-fashioned thing to do would be to publish it."'

So, with some initial financial backing from friends they struck out on their own and signed Fergus up. (He hasn't written his book yet, Jo confides – high-profile head gardeners are busy people these days, travelling the world lecturing and consulting and trying to write their books on planes.) But in 2015 they published their first gardening title, *Paradise and Plenty*, a gorgeously illustrated portrait by its designer Mary Keen of Lord Rothschild's private garden. It's a window into a dream, the kind of garden most of us will only ever set foot in as visitors. Soon after came *Landscape of Dreams*, a sumptuously produced gardening autobiography by Isabel and Julian Bannerman, garden designers known for what Prince Charles in his foreword calls their 'visionary creativity'. When the book was published a complimentary copy was dispatched to Birkhall, where HRH was on holiday. Jo tells me that soon after, she received a call from the courier saying he couldn't find Birkhall. 'I checked he'd got the postcode right, thinking, how many royal residences can there *be* in Aberdeenshire,' she says. 'In the end I phoned Clarence House, where someone suggested, "If all else fails, do you think they could find Balmoral? I'm sure the Queen would pass it on."'

But the list isn't all about posh gardeners and armchair gardening. There are plenty of books to assist and amuse the humbler gardener – what garden designer Mary Keen calls the 'How' as well as the 'Wow' – among them Griselda Kerr's *The Apprehensive Gardener*, a down-to-earth hand-holding practical beginner's guide; Clare Hastings's *Gardening Notes from a Late Bloomer*, a handbook on how to look after her beloved cottage garden when she's gone, addressed to her daughter Calypso; and Tim Richardson's no-nonsense *You Should Have Been Here Last Week: Sharp Cuttings from a Garden Writer*.

For the rest, the list is an eclectic mix of illustrated books on buildings and interiors, art and artists (Rex Whistler, Cedric Morris, Thomas Hennell), craft, cookery and design, veering off occasionally into byways such as 2017's bestselling *Posh Dogs* (melting photographs taken from the pages of *Country Life*). Most are originals, but some are rescued classics, including the cartoonist Osbert Lancaster's deliciously witty and satirical takes on the history of architecture, *Pillar to Post*, *Home Sweet Homes* and *Drayneflete Revealed*, which come as a set in an elegant slipcase under the title *Columns and Curlicues*.

On the face of it, it does seem miraculous that so many delectable-looking titles can issue from this one crowded room. But, as with many small independent businesses who can't afford to pay for workspace, Pimpernel is like an iceberg, with nine-tenths of it unseen. Working with Jo are Gail, Pimpernel's MD, who manages the business side ('and everything, really,' says Jo, fervently); Emma, who organizes publicity; Anna, who works with Jo on commissioning; Becky, their art director; Gill, the production manager, plus a network of freelance editors and designers, all of them beavering away at home. As I'm sitting on the sofa, leafing through another of the firm's bestsellers, *Seeking New York*, a journey through Manhattan's historic buildings and the sometimes gruesome stories attached to them, written by an Inspector in the auxiliary NYPD, one of the freelance editors drops in on her way back from seeing an author who's failing to deliver. 'I think the problem is he's a perfectionist and it's paralysing him. He needs a lot of support,' she observes sympathetically.

These are words to warm a writer's heart, and not so often heard these days in the offices of big publishers. As a result Pimpernel attracts books and authors who might easily have gone elsewhere. One such was Catherine Horwood with her recent biography of the legendary plantswoman Beth Chatto, eagerly awaited but revealing unknown aspects of its subject's life that kept it under wraps until after her death.

The attractively quirky nature of the Pimpernel list certainly tells you that it's based on personal taste and enthusiasm rather than decisions made round a boardroom table. Typical is the story of twin books by our own contributor, the distinguished biographer Michael Holroyd – *My Great Grandmother's Book of Ferns* and *My Aunt's Book of Silent Actors* – in which he traces the history of his family through a couple of serendipitous finds in the family attic. One was a collection, beautifully reproduced here, of pictures composed from exotic pressed ferns, of the kind often created by nineteenth-century colonial wives during their husbands' postings in India and other parts of the Empire. Jo found the idea irresistible, but labelling the ferns was a problem. After some difficulty they tracked down the world's greatest expert on Indian ferns, Christopher Fraser-Jenkins, who was found in a remote part of Nepal. He identified every frond, and was so fascinated by the project that he added his own anecdotes.

Though Pimpernel is unquestionably well connected, being a small publisher dealing in illustrated books that cost a lot to produce is a nail-biting business. A common publishing problem is overprinting, but misjudging a print run in the other direction is also a pitfall. One sumptuous book on a stately home which was predicted to have a relatively small sale, to everyone's surprise sold out before publication, with Amazon hoovering up the entire stock. Having no books to sell when the reviews come out can be very costly.

Yet, despite all the worries, and even if, as Jo laughingly puts it, Gail is checking the cash flow 'hourly', there's a fizz in the air at Pimpernel that is catching. This upbeat feeling apparently extends to both the authors and the reps, a notably cautious and sometimes world-weary group of people, who have to persuade bookshops to stock the books. 'My experience of sales conferences was that the reps were usually depressed,' says Jo, 'but ours are very jolly. They seem to really like the books.' Even the seasoned Michael Holroyd is on record as saying that Pimpernel is 'the best publisher in London – probably in the world'.

As I waited for a bus in the Harrow Road, a phrase used by Rebecca West in a long-ago review came into my head – 'life's golden overflow'. It could, I felt, be applied to the mission of Pimpernel, a small press celebrating those great civilizing elements – gardens, crafts, food, art, architecture, wit and humour – which help to make life worth living.

HAZEL WOOD loves her small garden but is still a very amateur gardener, anxious for all the information and inspiration she can get.

The illustrations by Osbert Lancaster in this article were reproduced in Clare Hastings's *Gardening Notes from a Late Bloomer.*

Blooming Marvellous

POLLY DEVLIN

Sometime in the late 1990s, when I was staying in Dublin with my sister Marie Heaney and her husband Seamus, he was working on the introduction to a book called *A Way of Life, Like Any Other*, which I took to be a novel. I'd never heard of it, but the fact that Seamus was writing an introduction to this new edition seemed like an honour and signalled importance. First published in 1977, it had won both the *Guardian* Fiction Prize and the American PEN/Hemingway Award. How had I missed it?

Seamus gave me some pages of his introduction to read and I remember being much taken by the author's use of the word 'cleanly' in a passage about acting as a carer for his father:

> I had been nearly two years caring for my father and had some reason to be pleased with my work. His habits were again cleanly, his house and its treasures were in order . . .

It was so simple, yet it marked him out as someone at home with what the poet Eavan Boland called 'that most fabulous of beasts, language'. The book's title originated in a flippant remark Seamus had once made in a Czech restaurant, which was seized upon by the author who – of course, of course! – happened to be there. The whole situation was somehow reminiscent of one of Flann O'Brien's delicious literary excursions poking fun at pretension. And appropriately the author's name was Darcy O'Brien, a moniker given him by

---

Darcy O'Brien, *A Way of Life, Like Any Other* (1977)
New York Review Books · Pb · 176pp · £12.99 · ISBN 9780940322790

Marguerite Churchill, his movie-star mother (a fabulously crazed, joyfully wicked, sexy creation, who didn't want anyone to think her son was common Irish. Jaysus, no.)

On New Year's Eve 2001, the worst snowstorm in England and Ireland for years closed nearly all the airports, but somehow one flight took off from Dublin to Bristol with Seamus and Marie on it. They made it to my house through the snowy Mendips where the rest of my family were waiting and hoping, and then through the hazardously high drifts to St Michael's church in Stinsford, Dorset, a place with special resonance for the Heaneys and for all of us because of our reverence for Thomas Hardy. We stood frozen amid the churchyard yews, wind howling, snow blasting down, as Seamus fulfilled a vow he had made years earlier to read aloud, over the poet's grave, that most confounding of autobiographical poems 'The Darkling Thrush', which Hardy had written there exactly one hundred years before.

> . . . An aged thrush, frail, gaunt and small,
> In blast be-ruffled plume,
> Had chosen thus to fling his soul
> Upon the growing gloom . . .

Later Seamus sent me a finished version of his introduction and a postcard with a watercolour of the graves of Hardy and his wives at St Michael's church which read: 'Polly – remembering your relish of the "cleanly" in Darcy's prose, I make bold to send you a copy of the introduction I eventually wrote. They've not sent me any copy of the book yet, but if they supply me, I'll forward one.' They did supply soon after and he sent it to me, but I avoided reading it, I don't know why. So years passed and Seamus died and broke our hearts, and after a while I took the book up and started to read.

*

From the first line – 'I would not change the beginning for anything'– I was laughing and in love. From this rocket launch we're propelled into the crazy realism of the world in which Darcy O'Brien grew up: Hollywood. His father George O'Brien had been a cowboy star of early cowboy movies and his mother 'a goddess of the silver screen' aka Marguerite Churchill, best remembered, if remembered at all, as John Wayne's leading lady in *The Big Trail*. She, in all her terrible beauty and drunkenness, a mini-Sarah Bernhardt in her theatrics, is the epicentre of Darcy's world, his scourge, his responsibility, his subject and source of love. This was not a novel, but then again, what was it? A sort of autobiography? A memoir? A fantasy? Whatever, it was in a class of its own and to use a catch-all word to describe it – picaresque, mercurial, cosmic, romantic, high-spirited (all true) – would limit its antic scope. 'I would pay hard cash, silver dollars on the barrelhead as the cowboy star father would have put it, to have written that first page of Darcy's first novel,' said his mentor, the novelist and Professor of English Literature at Berkeley, Thomas Flanagan. Here is the opening paragraph:

> I would not change the beginning for anything. I had an electric car, a starched white nanny, a pony, a bed modelled after that of Napoleon's son, and I was baptized by the Archbishop of the diocese. I wore hats and sucked on a little pipe. I was the darling of the ranch, pleasing everyone. One day I was sunning myself in the patio, lying out on the yellow and blue tiles, contemplating the geraniums and sniffing the hot, clean air. A bee came up and stung me on my bare fanny. The response to my screams was wonderful. Servants everywhere, my mother giving orders. Don Enrique applied an old Indian remedy and my father took me down to the beach house to let the salt water do its work. Oh, what a world it was! Was there ever so pampered an ass as mine?

O'Brien has a unique voice. Well, that's a given: writers have to have a unique voice. At times of course, given the subject – the coming of age, skipping disrespectfully towards a way of wisdom like any other – one hears Holden Caulfield mooching through the rye in the background, and James Joyce wittering away, but the final compact treasure chest that is this book is his alone. Not that he ever is. From childhood he is surrounded by the lunatic, wholly egocentric everyday society of Hollywood and he never misses a trick, that child ear of his attuned not just to audible nuance but to inaudible squeak.

His observation and remembrance of his hysterical Californian upbringing, his appetite for the absurd, his cynicism, his wit, the sheer intelligence blasting along had me panting with pleasure alongside. His encounter as an almost innocent 14-year-old with a pair of young hookers bought and paid for by his stepfather to divest him of his virginity is a work of subtext art in itself.

> 'Are you two related? You're not sisters or anything?'
> 'No.'
> 'How did you meet? Did you know each other before?'
> 'There's a guy we know,' Dot said.

There are passages where one might be inclined to say, as they do in Ireland, that he loses the run of himself and goes a wee bit Molly Bloomish, but since these too are sly examples of his erudition and a channelling of his literary hero, they are cherries on the confection. A confection with a solid bitter base flavoured with poignant dolorous detail but always lightly handled – his father's pained Catholicism, his mother's appallingly intimate confidences. Her way of life might well have sent her son haywire and perhaps it did – but what a joy his tightrope act on the loose line of sanity is. Below lie unnameable hurts, but he doesn't let us look down. The rapier work is in his dialogue. Here's his mother confiding to her young son about his new stepfather, Anatole, a Russian creation with certain similarities to Ivan the Terrible.

> 'He's a pig,' she said. 'I think he has Tartar blood.'
> 'I'm sorry,' I said.

> 'He's at me day and night. What does he expect?'
>
> 'It must be very difficult for you.'
>
> 'Difficult! The Whore of Babylon wouldn't put up with it! I don't know, dear, sometimes I think it's all just plain screwing. I don't think there's any love in it. Not that he means harm, the poor thing. I don't think he knows any better. He's had nothing but whores his whole life.'

Anatole is a man who stands out in a crowd, a hundred and eighty-five pounds of east European muscle, a compact rhino of a man, and a sculptor to boot:

> His Zeus assaulting Athene suggested far more than the obvious quest for union between the principles of creation and knowledge. The work achieved its effect of surprise and antic abandon through a single daring leap in construction; the goddess was five times the size of the father of the gods who, captured in the act of scrambling up the female buttocks, reflected in every straining sinew the desperation of a man who may have taken on a task too big for him.

When *A Way of Life, Like Any Other* – his first novel – was published in 1977, Darcy O'Brien was 28, already a professor at Pomona College in California, and author of three scholarly books – his doctoral thesis *The Conscience of James Joyce*, and monographs on the Irish poets W. R. Rodgers and Patrick Kavanagh. Later he became well-known for his award-winning true crime stories, among them *The Power to Hurt*, and *Two of a Kind: The Hillside Stranglers* which became a bestseller, was made into a television film and is now a standard text on criminology and psychology courses.

O'Brien's interest in Ireland and Irish literature was aroused by Thomas Flanagan when he was a postgraduate student at Berkeley. It was Flanagan who showed him that his academic WASP background (Princeton and a Fulbright scholarship to Cambridge) and his Irish heritage could be brought into creative alignment, and he began his annual pilgrimages to Ireland. I never met him and wish I had, but Seamus described him as tanned, seersuckered, elegantly shod and shoe-shined. 'He'd arrive in Ireland every summer and move like a Californian Apollo through the bohemian kitchens of Dublin and Connemara.' From 1978 to 1995 he was a popular Professor in the English Department at Tulsa University. He was only 58 when, crowned with awards, fellowships and honours, he died of a heart attack in 1998.

Seamus never did quite make up his mind over whether *A Way of Life, Like Any Other* was an autobiographical novel or a fictionalized memoir, a *cri de coeur* or a comic turn – it was all of these things and more – a joy to read, what T. S. Eliot called 'the complete consort dancing together'.

And his introduction? A dazzling bonus, every sentence revealing Seamus's sweet tooth for irony, wit, humour and language. 'A jubilation, a ventriloquism, a writer figure-skating into his kingdom, his self-awareness, his release. Hollywood is there in all its crazy realism, autobiography is there in all its poignant detail, but what is chiefly present is a sense of the language performing in and for and through the writer.'

I couldn't have said it better myself.

POLLY DEVLIN's latest book is *Writing Home*, a sort of accidental memoir. She lives in London and sometimes teaches at Barnard College, Columbia University, in New York.

The Force of History

TIM PEARS

> My father once told me that our history is like a force behind us, pushing us along, unacknowledged or even unknown, but dictating the way we live our lives.

In the Memory of the Forest by Charles T. Powers is set in a small Polish town fifty miles east of Warsaw in the early 1990s. Communism is being dismantled. Free-market capitalism lets rip.

The body of a young man, Tomek Powierza, is found in the forest, victim of foul play. The police chief is incompetent. Other officials hamper Tomek's father, Staszek's, attempts to investigate. His neighbour, the young farmer Leszek Maleszewski, helps him. They discover murky business deals with Russian gangs, in which Tomek was involved, deals conducted by ex-Communist officials, hanging on to any kind of power in the new world order.

Meanwhile other forces are at work. Church authorities allocate elderly Father Tadeusz a fierce new curate, who leads a campaign to purge the town leadership of its Communist stain. But such purification is not so simple. Young Father Jerzy uncovers evidence that a previous incumbent had a fine new rectory built with the Party's help, but finds that the Bishopric is less impressed by his zeal than he had expected.

Leszek's investigation into Tomek's death threatens the local Party head, who retaliates with names from the town's extensive list of informers: they include not only Leszek's own father, but also the

---

Charles T. Powers, *In the Memory of the Forest* (1997), is out of print but we can obtain second-hand copies.

vet with whose wife he is conducting a naïve, first-love affair.

She tells Leszek, 'It's worse since the changes. Karol said it would be this way. He's right. It's just as rotten. Only now we have the privilege of smelling it.'

Then people discover in the mornings that stones have been dug out from the foundations of their barns and outbuildings. They begin to ask, 'Are they coming back?'

'Who are they?' Leszek wonders. 'The Jews,' he is told. He learns for the first time that once many Jews lived in the town; they were rounded up and taken away by the Nazis. Then other townspeople took over their homes, and used stones from the Jewish cemetery to build new barns.

And thus Charles T. Powers weaves a tapestry of interconnecting explorations of corruption and collusion, of the past buried yet with the present rooted in it. Everyone is implicated in one way or another, and now everyone is guilty and suspicious and paranoid.

The American author had been a journalist for the *Los Angeles Times*, and was Eastern European Bureau Chief based in Warsaw from 1986 to 1991. He then returned to the States and wrote the novel over the following five years – during which time he developed cancer. He died at the age of 53 in 1996, shortly after completing the book. It was published posthumously in 1997, to glowing reviews.

*

I read *In the Memory of the Forest* in 1998, shortly before I married a woman who is half-Polish. Her father Paul was a man I admired enormously. He came to Britain as a refugee in 1948, at the age of 19, his few clothes and possessions contained in a British Army kit bag slung over his shoulder. The war had robbed him of his youth and education; the subsequent Soviet occupation of Poland robbed him of a home. He told his children little about his childhood or his experiences in the war. He never took them to Poland or taught them Polish.

In London he worked in a factory while he studied Algebra, Geometry and Trigonometry by correspondence, and took evening classes in mechanical draughtsmanship. In 1955 he got a job in Engineering Research and Development at Metal Box – where he would remain for the rest of his working life, becoming a Senior Designing Engineer.

Paul met and married an Englishwoman, Ann, in 1961. They had three children: two boys sandwiching a girl, Hania. But Paul's fierce determination did not make for domestic harmony. The man who'd lost so much held too tight. His marriage to Ann floundered; his children became increasingly alienated.

*

In his novel Charles T. Powers weaves a tapestry of threads tying the present to the past, then he carefully unpicks it. 'Farm work is reality,' Leszek says,

> but as the ax sank into wood and the wrench slipped on the grease-caked nuts in the tractor's engine, solid objects under my grip gave no hold against the overwhelming sense of being surrounded by memories, misinterpretations, and illusions weeded and tended as carefully as a kitchen garden . . . All around me, memories recurred; like stones in a path, they pushed up. Memory had a future as well as a past.

The novel is written with a scrupulous clarity; with great intelligence but not knowingness. There is an innocence in its lucid style, reminiscent of Isaac Bashevis Singer.

> Here were the gargoyle faces of men standing in doorways, drunkenness working at them like magnified gravity, tugging flesh earthward, slowing words and motion. An old woman, gray as bone, veered wide around them, tugging her tiny frightened dog.

It's a wonderfully told story of the past rising from hidden graves to shame the present, and it burns with a mounting moral force. Though young Leszek narrates alternate chapters, old Father Tadeusz emerges as its moral centre. He realizes he 'had sought to muffle himself against his surroundings', but gradually he faces up to the past, and obliges his parishioners to do the same.

*

Hania and I both read *In the Memory of the Forest* as we planned our marriage, and honeymoon. Hania wanted to go to Poland for the first time. Her father suggested meeting us there, to show her where he was born. So Hania and I drove through Belgium, Germany and the Czech Republic, heading towards the centre of Europe. We reached Tylicz, a small village in the forested foothills of the Carpathians, in the south of Poland, very close to the Slovakian border, where Paul was born on 8 February 1928. He was the seventh of nine children born to Maria and Michal, a forester. Only four children survived infancy or childhood.

Over the following days we visited the houses, churches and schools, the fields and forests, of Paul's childhood. Over meals of bigos and pierogi, over coffees and beers, he told his daughter (and attendant son-in-law) his story for the first time.

Paul was 11 in September 1939 when the German Wehrmacht and Luftwaffe invaded and then occupied Poland. In late 1943 Germany feared attack from its erstwhile Soviet ally. Paul and his younger brother Teodor were pressed into child labour gangs to dig a line of trenches against Soviet tanks. Teodor was then allowed to go home, but Paul, by now aged 15, was sent to Germany. There, through 1944 and into 1945, he worked as a forced labourer, repairing and clearing the rubble of cities being bombed from the air.

There was little food. During Allied air raids, when the German guards ran for the nearest shelter, Paul rushed in the opposite direction, into fields where he scrabbled up potatoes or carrots with his hands and ate them raw. Early in 1945, a wall collapsed on him. His leg was broken, and he was put in a cellar with straw on the floor along with other injured workers, and left to heal or die. Occasionally a brave German civilian would pass a loaf of bread through the grille at pavement level.

In April 1945 Paul was in Bavaria when it was conquered by American troops. For the next two and a half years he was employed by the US Government as a driver in Schweinfurt, where he learned car mechanics.

He wondered where to go now. Back to Poland? But from his family there came no reply to his letters. Furthermore, he understood it was dangerous to return to what was now the Stalinist Polish People's Republic. Anyone tainted by contact with the West was liable to deportation to camps in the USSR.

And so he took the opportunity to come to Britain. It would be another twenty years before the Red Cross located his mother and his younger brother Teodor, living in Lviv, a city which had been in eastern Poland but was now in Ukraine. He never saw either of his parents alive again, and it wasn't until the '70s that he felt able to go to see Teodor and meet his brother's Ukrainian wife, Katia, and their children.

Paul told us much yet still held something back. I couldn't imagine what it was, but then Hania asked her father a question: he had a younger brother, Teodor. But four children had survived infancy. What had happened to his other two siblings?

Paul said nothing for a long time. Neither did his daughter. Then he took a deep breath, as if he needed to really fill his lungs to be able to share his story. He told us how in occupied Poland there was an escape route for Poles through the forests and over the border into Slovakia, through Hungary and onwards. His older brother Basyli was a people smuggler for the Polish underground. In 1942, during such an operation, he and his comrades were intercepted by the Germans and shot.

Hania and I took a trek into the forest. Weirdly, we unwittingly crossed the Slovak border and suddenly found ourselves surrounded by armed soldiers, who must have been out on exercise, and redirected us back towards Poland.

It was the next day that Paul told us of his beloved elder sister Maria. He learned after the war that she had been killed by Soviet soldiers, on a train, in circumstances that he would or could not elaborate upon. But we knew what Red Army soldiers did to women across Europe.

As Paul told Hania the story of his youth, shedding light thereby on his later achievements and his failings, I understood that the woman I'd just married brought her family history with her.

Paul died in 2013. In the last weeks of his life, in the John Radcliffe and Churchill hospitals in Oxford, he was treated by three senior doctors: Dr Mason, an Englishman; Dr Fliettner, a German; and Dr Darowski, a Pole. Given his life story, it seemed appropriate.

My wife studied history at Oxford – the first from either side of her family to go to university. She spent her twenties doing different things. When we met she was a dance teacher. After our children were born, she retrained, and eventually became a psychoanalyst. Now she helps people explore their own histories – the unique personal and political legacy that each of us owns. For as one of Powers's characters in his novel says:

> My father once told me that our history is like a force behind us, pushing us along, unacknowledged or even unknown, but dictating the way we live our lives.

TIM PEARS's most recent novels are the West Country trilogy: *The Horseman*, *The Wanderers* and *The Redeemed*. He also loves writing about sport and politics.

Mood Music

LAURA FREEMAN

'Dance after dance with an old fogey. Three running now, pressed to his paunch.' Oh, the hell of parties! The small humiliations. The shy, smudged-mascara, wallflower-grief of it all. Where was Rollo? Archie? Tony? Even Reggie, dreaded Reggie, would do. In Rosamond Lehmann's *Invitation to the Waltz* we share every agony, every spurning, every smallest saving grace with Olivia Curtis, just 17 and, as her dressmaker cheerfully tells her, 'no bewtee'. We meet her on her birthday, staring into the bedroom mirror with a mix of adolescent pride and doubt. And such is Lehmann's uncanny power that the reflection in the glass isn't Olivia's: it's our own.

'Dear Miss Lehmann, How *did* you know? This is my story exactly.' So wrote reader after reader to the 26-year-old Lehmann when her first novel *Dusty Answer*, about first love, first university terms, first friendships with girls more glamorous than oneself, became a 'terrifying' success. Lehmann catches the voice of the young woman trembling between girlhood and sophistication. Judith in *Dusty Answer* and Olivia in *Invitation to the Waltz* are hesitant, resolute, gauche and vain. Olivia asks when – *when?* – will her life begin. Yet, when drunk, boorish Archie forgets he has marked his dance card with her name, she thinks: 'It can't be true. It's too much. How can I live if things like this are going to happen?'

Invitation to the Waltz is a book not just about going to a party, but about how going to a party, when you've never been to one

---

Rosamond Lehmann, *Invitation to the Waltz* (1932)
Virago · Pb · 256pp · £9.99 · ISBN 9781844083053

before, can mark the moment between callow childhood and adolescent assurance. The experience offers Olivia a tantalizing glimpse of the future with all its promised tragedy, romance and conquest.

There are three parts to the *Waltz*. We hear the orchestra tuning up as we see Olivia and her older sister Kate (now Kate *is* a 'bewtee') preparing, powdering, pinning, pining, dreaming of the dance at the Spencers'. They worry about knicker lines and bodices and whether their seams will show. They agonize about Not Knowing Any Boys. Then comes the party, thrown by Sir John and Lady Spencer for their son Rollo and daughter Marigold, a schoolroom friend of Olivia's, who is wearing a 'fascinating frock' sent by her godmother from Paris. The third and final movement sees Olivia and Kate safely back home. As they pour cocoa from a Thermos, the sisters yawn and ask: Did I enjoy myself?

We know, even if Kate, who can think only of Tony, has forgotten to ask, whether or not Olivia has enjoyed her evening. It was hell – 'Bombshells. Death and damnation . . . Consternation. Humiliation.' And it was rapture – alone with Rollo on the terrace, talking together about books. 'She hadn't felt so happy all the evening. Such an interesting, serious conversation.' She is taken by Rollo to meet his father. 'Here's another recluse,' says Rollo. 'She's a great reader, Daddy . . . You can't catch her out. Every one of your pet classics.' Not a bewtee, but a brain. And that is better, surely? Better to talk about Dickens and Thackeray and Eliot and Austen with clever Rollo than be Kate gazing into Tony's eyes as he tells her, 'You'd look corking on a horse.' Every minute of the evening is an eternity – and it is all over in an ecstatic instant.

I first read Rosamond Lehmann after I broke bounds. It was at the Chipping Norton Literary Festival where I was due to appear with Lucy Mangan. We had both written books about books – *The Reading Cure* and *Bookworm* – and had been registered, hustled into the green room and told to stay put. Festivals are frightened of losing authors. Once they have you, they don't like to let you go until you've made it on to the stage, spoken and signed a dozen books. But Lucy had heard that the Oxfam bookshop in Chipping Norton was a good one and so, twenty minutes before our slot, we bolted. On the principle that you should always 'Pick up a Penguin', I bought Rosamond Lehmann's *The Echoing Grove.*

Over the following weeks, slyly, secretively, rather in the manner of an affair, I read *The Echoing Grove* (1953), *The Weather in the Streets* (1936), *Invitation to the Waltz* (1932) and *Dusty Answer* (1927) – all in the wrong order. I say an affair because Lehmann's books have a clandestine feel, like the sharing of a secret. Sometimes you draw back – *I shouldn't have pried, forgive me . . .* Sometimes you lean in – *Go on. I won't tell a soul . . .*

Howard Coster (© NPG)

Olivia Curtis isn't Rosamond Lehmann, but there are similarities. Olivia is a 'secretive adolescent' given to sitting in the walnut tree in her parents' garden with a notebook, pencil and bag of caramels. Lehmann, from the age of 8, would balance in the fork of her own walnut tree, writing plays, poems and epics which she remembered in rueful adulthood as coming to her in torrents of sentimental inspiration: 'heather, weather, brim, dim, bloom, gloom and off we go: every rhyme rhyming, every fairy flitting, stars glimmering, moon beaming, wind sighing, buds breaking'. Her mother Alice, the author said, had subtle ways of 'deflating vanity'. Once, Alice overheard the young Rosamond boasting to a group of family friends about her poetic gifts. Alice interrupted her daughter with: 'Rosie writes doggerel.' Lehmann said her mother's words 'went through me like a sword-thrust'.

Like Olivia, Rosamond was a middle child, the second of four, a position she described in her short story 'The Red-haired Miss Daintreys' as 'like the jam in a sandwich. Snug.' They were a literary family. Her great-grandfather Robert Chambers was co-founder of Chambers, the publishing firm, her father Rudolph Chambers Lehmann founded *Granta*, wrote for *Punch* and edited the *Daily News*. Her younger brother John Lehmann was a poet, publisher and editor of Penguin *New Writing*. (He bought Virginia Woolf's share of the Hogarth Press and described their often prickly partnership in *Thrown to the Woolfs* (1978).)

There's a younger brother, James, who plays a small but beautifully observed part in *Invitation to the Waltz*. But this is a book about sisters. Since I have only a brother I have often tested out literary sisterhoods. Jo and Meg in *Little Women*? Elinor and Marianne in *Sense and Sensibility*? Pauline, Petrova and Posy in *Ballet Shoes*? Would I have liked sisters like that? Only Olivia and Kate have felt completely real: practical, fond, disapproving, liable to squabble. Reading the scene in which Kate and Olivia sit at opposite ends of the bath before the party – Nannie has run the water and laid out the towels – soaking in Heart-of-a-Rose salts, I can't help thinking: how lucky to have a sister, someone to tell you your dress is on back to front, to keep you company in cabs, to say: 'Sh! Be quiet. Don't think about it' when you tell them your insides have turned to nervous water.

The Spencers' party is a fiasco and a triumph. Olivia is buttonholed by a morbid, half-drunk poet who lectures her on modern verse and refuses to ask her to dance. She is introduced to a blind soldier who had wanted to be an architect before the war but now keeps chickens with a dumpy wife who was his nurse. As he dances with Olivia he steps on her feet. You can't read this scene without tears. Lehmann makes Olivia's partner stand for every young man who fought in the First World War and was injured in body and spirit. Rollo's older brother Guy never came home. But for Olivia Rollo redeems all. A few moments talking about *Tom Jones* and *Tristram Shandy*, and all those shameful hours hiding in the cloakroom, hovering in corridors, sitting out dances without partners are as nothing.

An hour before the party Olivia, dressed and smelling a little too strongly of Lily of the Valley, bumps into her Uncle Oswald in the upstairs corridor. 'Oh . . . I'm all wrong,' she bursts out. 'I know I am.' Her red silk is cutting in at the armpits, her hair is pulled back too tight. 'Never mind,' Uncle Oswald whispers to her. 'You must just wait. Say another ten years . . . It all quiets down. Yes. It gets better. Don't worry. You'll be all right in the end.' It is the proper advice for a girl on the eve of her first ball.

In *The Weather in the Streets*, set ten years after the Spencers' party, we meet Olivia at the moment forecast by Uncle Oswald. Now Kate is married – though not to Tony – with four flourishing children. Good, dependable, sensible, irritable Kate, a 'fresh young matron from the country' Olivia calls her older sister, trying to wind her up. So what can one say about Olivia? She is too thin. She is an assistant to a photographer. She is separated – though not divorced – from her husband Ivor. She has only 1s 6d left in her purse.

In the novel's opening scene, Olivia is summoned home to say goodbye to her ailing father. Frantic, fearful, wondering if she ought to buy black gloves, she rushes for the train at Paddington. The man opposite her in the carriage, ordering sausages, scrambled eggs, coffee, toast and marmalade and half-hidden behind *The Times*, is . . . Rollo. I won't spoil it. But Uncle Oswald was wrong. Life doesn't quieten down. It is here, in the breakfast car as the train pulls away through the London fog, talking once again about books with Rollo Spencer, that for Olivia the dance really begins.

LAURA FREEMAN is gladder than she can say that she is no longer 17. She hopes one day to grow out of hiding in the cloakroom at parties.

An Irresistible Cad

ANTHONY GARDNER

Is it possible to love a book and hate it at the same time? That is the question that nags me whenever I think of Guy de Maupassant's novel *Bel-Ami* (1885). It's undoubtedly a masterpiece: the characterization is subtle, the social critique is incisive, the plot is completely absorbing. But its protagonist, nicknamed Bel-Ami because of his extraordinary good looks, is one of literature's most despicable creations: a man who tramples on friend and foe alike – and above all on the women who love him – in his pursuit of wealth and status. With another writer, you might stomach such behaviour in the sure expectation of a spectacular come-uppance; but Maupassant's amoral universe is one in which some people can get away with anything. What keeps us turning the pages is the brilliance of his writing and a fascination with how far his anti-hero can go.

When we first meet George Duroy he is a young man on his uppers in 1880s Paris. The son of peasant innkeepers, he's spent two and a half years with the army in North Africa, and has come to the city to seek his fortune; but all he's found so far is a badly paid job as a railway clerk. As he wanders the streets on a warm summer evening, he longs for a glass of beer but knows he'll have to go hungry if he buys one.

Then, among the crowd, he spots an old comrade. Charles Forestier has become the political editor of a newspaper, *La Vie Française*, and suggests that his friend too should try journalism. To

---

Guy de Maupassant, *Bel-Ami* (1885) · Trans. Margaret Mauldon
OUP · Pb · 368pp · £8.99 · ISBN 9780199553938

help him on his way, he invites him to dinner to meet the paper's owner, Monsieur Walter. When Duroy admits that he doesn't have any suitable clothes, Forestier lends him the money to hire some: in Paris, he advises, appearances are everything. 'You're better off without a bed than without evening clothes.'

At the dinner Duroy meets three women who will fall under his spell and advance his career: Forestier's beautiful young wife Madeleine; her friend Clothilde de Marelle, whose husband's frequent business trips leave her free to pursue an affair; and the pious, middle-aged Madame Walter. All in different ways will be betrayed.

Madeleine Forestier is the book's most enigmatic and intriguing character. A thoroughly modern woman, from her cigarette-smoking to her insistence on leading an independent life, she's a journalist manquée who ghosts her husband's articles and has her own highly effective network of political informants. Duroy recognizes her as exactly the kind of wife an ambitious man needs, and, when Forestier develops a fatal illness, loses no time in offering himself as a replacement. How exactly Madeleine feels about Duroy – whether there's an element of calculation as well as love in her acceptance of him – we are never allowed to know, but Maupassant suggests that she is more alert to his machinations than anyone else. When Duroy tries to persuade her to make a large sum of money over to him, the author reflects on the mystery within every marriage:

> He stopped in front of her; and once again they stood for a few moments staring into each other's eyes, each striving to uncover the impenetrable secret of the other's heart, to touch the quick of their mind. In an intense, silent cross-examination they tried to see each other's soul laid bare – the intimate struggle of two beings who, living side by side, remain for ever closed to one another . . .

Maupassant draws us into his tale with all the skill of an angler playing a fish, allowing us spells of sympathy for Duroy before tugging us back to face the unpalatable truth. Above all, he exploits our love of rags-to-riches stories and our instinctive support for the underdog. Duroy's rise is swift, but he's made to suffer along the way. With no natural gift for writing, he agonizes over his articles and endures a dogsbody apprenticeship on *La Vie Française* until Madame Walter secures his promotion; he's often humiliatingly short of money; and he lives in fear of making a terrible faux pas. When, after sitting tongue-tied in the corner of a smart salon, he finally manages a remark that wins approval, we can't help delighting in his triumph.

And yet it's plain from the first few pages that he's a reprobate. Leaving a cheap restaurant, he casts a predatory eye over the female diners, calculating the effect of his looks on them; half of the money Forestier lends him is immediately spent on a prostitute. Worst of all, he remembers with 'a cruel, gleeful smile' the loot he collected in Africa on a raid that cost three tribesmen their lives.

Maupassant, though, won't allow us the luxury of believing that Duroy is altogether different from us. He's capable of spontaneous acts of kindness, such as playing with Clothilde de Marelle's withdrawn daughter, Laurine – the person who christens him Bel-Ami. And some of the temptations he falls into are common enough: when he finds himself penniless and Clothilde gives him money, he swears that he will repay her but gradually persuades himself that this isn't really necessary.

Maupassant shows above all that Duroy is the product of a specific society: *fin-de-siècle* Paris in all its decadence. Of those he encounters, Madame Walter alone is beyond reproach – and even she is eventually corrupted. Clothilde has no qualms about betraying her husband; Forestier and his colleagues at *La Vie Française* have little interest in truth or morality. The newspaper, indeed, exists mainly to promote the business interests of its proprietor, who makes a vast fortune by a spectacular act of deceit with the aid of a corrupt politician. Duroy, writing leaders about the decline of morals, may be a hypocrite, but he's one among many.

My addiction to Maupassant began with a desperate need to brush up my French. Searching the family bookshelves on the eve of a Eurostar expedition, I came across a collection of his short stories which, with their compelling storylines and elegant but straightforward language, fitted the bill perfectly. Now, whenever I find myself in Paris, I try to visit a splendid bookshop on the Boulevard St Germain and buy another neat little paperback in the Livre de Poche series; and having graduated from the short stories to the novels, I find it impossible to picture that part of the city without Bel-Ami strolling through it. But you don't have to cross the Channel or own a dictionary to enjoy the novel; the best translation I've found is Margaret Mauldon's for Oxford World's Classics.

In *Bel-Ami*, you sense the master of the short story wanting to make the most of his wider canvas, and it includes a number of extended set pieces which are highly readable but not always essential to the plot, such as the scene in which Duroy finds himself forced to fight a duel.

> The conversation faltered, despite the anecdotes that the doctor trotted out. Only Rival made any reply. Duroy would have liked to join in, just to show a degree of coolness, but he was afraid of losing his train of thought, of betraying the desperate anxiety that he felt – and he was haunted by the excruciating fear that he might start to tremble.
>
> Soon the carriage was in open countryside. It was around nine o'clock. It was one of those bitterly cold winter mornings on which all of nature is as dazzling and as brittle as crystal. The trees seem to have sweated ice, leaving them covered in hoarfrost; the ground rings with every footstep; the dry air carries the slightest noise far into the distance; the blue sky shines as brightly as a mirror, and the sun – itself cold and dazzling – moves through the firmament pouring down rays that warm nothing on to the frozen world.

Maupassant's account of Forestier's lingering death is masterful and chilling, and he finds room for a long disquisition on mortality by an elderly poet, Norbert de Varenne. But even this can only throw Duroy momentarily off his stride: he and Varenne have barely parted company when a woman's perfume reminds him of life's sensual pleasures, and he returns to his old ways.

What drives Duroy above all is a hatred of those who have more than he does. At his most penurious, he rages at the men he sees sitting in cafés:

> On average, each must have at least forty francs; there were at least a hundred of them in each café; a hundred times forty made four thousand francs. 'The swine!' he muttered . . . If he'd been able to grab any one of them on a street corner, deep in the shadows, he would have wrung his neck without a second thought . . .

By the end of the novel 4,000 francs will be small change to Duroy, and Maupassant hints that he will go on to make his mark in politics. It's such a deplorable state of affairs that I wonder if I can bear to read *Bel-Ami* again – but something tells me that I won't be able to resist it.

ANTHONY GARDNER's grandparents were so keen on French that it was the only language they allowed to be spoken in their house on Wednesdays. Some felt that this was asking a bit much of the cook. He is the author of two novels, *The Rivers of Heaven* and *Fox*, and a collection of poetry, *The Pool and Other Poems*.

Going Loco

MARTIN SORRELL

Recently, lingering in my loft over books and back numbers of this journal and that, I stumbled on a photo of some schoolboys, paper and pencils in hand, sitting on a fence and watching a train go by. The location was Tring; the date, 1933. It's a safe bet that what those lads were jotting down was the number of the steam locomotive at the head of the express.

That date, 1933, surprised me. I'd always thought that loco-spotting – collecting engine numbers as if they were physical entities, like stamps or butterflies – wasn't invented until a decade later, when a 20-year-old clerk in the Southern Railway's publicity department hit upon an idea, one that would make his name and fortune. Ian Allan had been spared military service courtesy of an amputated leg, and had been entrusted with a swelling postbag of requests for information about the Southern's locomotives. His idea was to issue a booklet listing the hundreds of engines the company owned, and sell it for a shilling.

It was an immediate hit. It told the purchaser – doubtless roughly 98 per cent male – whether a particular locomotive was large or medium or puny, whether used on passenger or freight trains or to shunt things around, whether to be found on main or branch lines or in sidings. The identification numbers they carried were printed in sequence, columns of figures down the page, asking to be ticked or

---

A whole host of books on Britain's trains, including reissues of some *Combined ABC*s, are available from Ian Allan Ltd. See their website www.ianallanpublishing.com.

underlined. As indeed they would be by a myriad schoolboys and, it was said, several vicars and the odd bishop. Thus, with one simple stroke of commercial genius, was born a book of numbers that launched several decades' worth of the *Ian Allan ABC of British Locomotives*, the loco-spotters' bible.

I've never seen that first *ABC*, but I'd like to think that Mr Allan enriched his list with the names the Southern gave their most glamorous engines: *King Arthur*, *Queen Guinevere*, *Camelot*, *Maid of Astolat*, *Excalibur*, *Lord Nelson*, *Sir Walter Raleigh*, *Howard of Effingham* . . . But, with or without those names, Allan's pioneer booklet of 1942 kick-started a national craze. Kick-started, because evidently the craze had long been gathering steam on stations and fences in Tring and everywhere else. And what a craze! It may have quietened down now, but in the mid-1950s, when I was growing up, there can't have been more than seven or eight boys in any classroom of thirty plus who didn't talk trains and numbers (when not busy recreating the latest *Goon Show*, our other obsession). Spotting was the perfect hobby in those post-war years of make-do, because it could be indulged in for free; the minimum requirements were an exercise book and a pencil, both 'borrowable' from school. Plus access to a railway line, of course. But most of us acquired at least one of the *Ian Allan ABC*s which had been hitting the market since the late 1940s.

By that time Allan's original list had spawned a series of booklets illustrated with black-and-white photos. There was one booklet for each region of Britain's newly nationalized railways. As our school was in Sussex, the *ABC* of choice was the *Southern*. The *pièce de résistance*, however, was the *Combined Volume*; every engine number in the UK contained in one compact hardback. When finally I got to own one, I spent a happy half-hour covering it in protective brown paper and inscribing it in dodgy italics. At 10s 6d, the *Combined* didn't come cheap: though that's 53 pence in today's money, it's nowhere near the true cost. When I cycled to Thakeham at weekends to pick mushrooms for four solid hours in a sunless shed sans tea-break, I was paid off with a ten-shilling note.

New *ABC*s came out every year or two. They needed to, because locomotives were constantly falling off the record, scrapped or put in store for a rainy day, as happened when the hapless post-Beeching diesels kept collapsing. And steam locomotives were still being built in the '50s and so had to be added to the tally. For me, that was of extra interest, as one design – a handsome tank engine – was being built in large quantities at the nearby Brighton Works, and each new example was tried out on my branch line. More numbers to harvest.

The spotter's basic objective was to *cop* – see for the first time – as many locomotives as possible and note down their numbers. Now I look back on it, it does seem a batty idea to 'collect' something as arbitrary and insubstantial as a number on metal. Especially as what it denoted was not fixed for life but comprised an assembly of parts constantly getting changed. Boilers, wheels and much else would be swapped around with equivalents from sister engines. A thorny issue of identity, then. What exactly *were* we spotting?

And why did we do it? Perhaps, as Everest was for Mallory, just because those engines were there – and because they *weren't* there. There was no guarantee that a locomotive we were seeking would ever materialize. That of course only increased the thrill of the hunt, which is what loco-spotting was about, as birding is for some twitchers. But what joy it was to cop an especially elusive engine, as happened to me one August afternoon on Andover station when an express thundered past, headed by the gleaming green *Shaftesbury*, the one member of its class I still hadn't spotted. I yelped with the emotion of it, jumped up and down and, tearful with gratitude, raised my arms in salute to the locomotive's unseen crew.

I don't recall whether at that stage I was in possession of the crucial annex to the *ABC*s which Ian Allan Ltd, as it now was, had started to produce: the *Locoshed Book*. It was like the *ABC* in that every engine number was listed, but the extra detail provided was the identity of each one's home depot, where it was *shedded*. Every shed in the land had its code number: nearest to my village was 75A, Brighton. In effect, the *Locoshed Book* was a coded map; but it was also an atlas for the imagination, the way railway timetables were for Proust. Armed with it, I did what the sickly Proust couldn't, I planned and executed complicated journeys of well over 300 miles in a day. The aim as ever was to cop new engines, among them *namers* rarer even than *Shaftesbury*.

Namers: giving names to locomotives seems to be mostly a British quirk. It still goes on. Stand by any main line today and before long you'll see at least one diesel or electric locomotive with a nameplate bolted to its flanks. But the choice of name! It's odds on that it will be of a power station or a freight depot. So much for imagination, then. Gone are the brass plates proclaiming *Shooting Star* and *Golden Fleece*, *Ivanhoe* and *Owen Glendower* . . . But hold on, let's not get too dewy-eyed. The publicity people in the Good Old Days could also get it wrong. Think only of the world's fastest steam locomotive, a beautiful streamlined masterpiece of the 1930s; it was named after a duck – *Mallard!*

On the very last day of the 1950s, my family moved from our house by a Sussex branch line, and within a couple of years I was starting university. Determined never to be thought uncool, I steered clear of the city's station, ironically the best location in the country to see locomotives from every region except Scotland. And I sold my railway stuff to a fellow inmate of my college, a cheery extrovert with no hang-ups about loving trains. But I wish I'd kept my *ABC*s at least. They'd have been the most potent of aide-memoires.

And I realize now how educational they were, more than I knew at the time. Those strings of numbers, of no value in themselves, unlike stamp and butterfly collections, were keys that opened doors to geography, history, legend, and more besides. Among the rewards of my number-chases was the discovery of fifty-four Knights of the Round Table, sixteen admirals of the fleet, forty public schools, sixty-six West Country towns and places, several outposts of the fading Empire, and a few characters from Wales's and Scotland's distant past. More importantly still, loco-spotting taught me and my generation to be independent, to journey alone, read maps and timetables, use our initiative, nurture the imagination. And exist on corned beef sandwiches.

These days, I check charity shops for old *ABC*s. They're difficult to find, especially the original *Combined* of the dates I want, the mid-50s. The closest I've come is a damaged *Combined* of 1961. Several pages have been torn out. Why, I can't fathom. Still, it's better than nothing, even though its first owner's underlinings coincide with hardly a single locomotive I ever saw. But this honeycomb of a book will have to do for now, the half-glimpsed record of another person's past.

MARTIN SORRELL eventually realized a boyhood ambition when he drove the *Flying Scotsman*, no less. It cost him 371 *Combined ABC*s but was worth every penny.

Coal, Rent and Chaos

MICHAEL LEAPMAN

A couple of years ago the judges for the Bollinger Everyman Wodehouse prize for comic fiction decided that none of the sixty-two books submitted was funny enough to win, so they withheld the award. One of them, the publisher David Campbell, explained: 'Despite the submitted books producing many a wry smile amongst the panel during the judging process, we did not feel than any of the books we read this year incited the level of unanimous laughter we have come to expect.' Humour is notoriously subjective, but I am confident that if the prize had existed sixty-seven years ago, Gwyn Thomas's *A Frost on My Frolic* would have been a strong contender.

Thomas, who died in 1981 aged 67, was a popular writer in the Fifties and became a minor television personality; yet he is scarcely remembered today. His readers could certainly look forward to both wry smiles and guffaws, before being pulled up short by some searing emotional or political outburst that conveyed a more serious intent: the frost on his frolics. With a style rooted in his native Wales, he shared with Wodehouse a gift for creating strong characters and examining closely – in unorthodox, imaginative and often hilarious language – how they reacted to the extreme situations in which he placed them; albeit that the worlds the two authors chronicled are at opposite poles of the social scale. While 'the poor man's Wodehouse' is not a characterization Thomas would have relished or even recognized, it is, in a literal sense, applicable to at least some of his writing.

Gwyn Thomas, *A Frost on My Frolic* (1953), is out of print, but we can obtain second-hand copies.

Contemporary critics gave him rave reviews. John Betjeman lauded his 'heavenly gift of amusing description'. Howard Spring detected in him 'the gusto of genius'. Lionel Hale declared: 'There is poetry in him – even the fun is poetical.' And reviewing *A Frost on My Frolic*, published by Gollancz in 1953, John Connell called Thomas 'a comic genius whose work takes you by the throat and shakes you with laughter, wonder, joy and gratitude'.

My copy carries an inscription revealing that I acquired it in August 1955, when I was 17. I must have bought it from a second-hand shop, since the green 'Boots Booklovers [no apostrophe] Library' shield on the cover has been properly cancelled with a heavy printed X: evidence that I had not simply forgotten to return it to the local branch. Although it is in no sense targeted at teenagers, what probably appealed to me at first was that its principal characters are a group of youths in their last year at school, as I was – and the description of the school's location on the first page would certainly have taken me by the throat:

> My friend Spencer and I walk up the hill towards the school. We bend forward to make the hill seem less steep. This is our fifth year at the school and our thoughts about this slope have grown more plentiful and profound with the passing of each month. No doubt the governing body and their friends have heard of such schools as Harrow which are also built on hills and thought, by hoisting this one on its present perch, to give Mynydd Coch, which is as rough a place as you will find in this sector, a better tone. But those young elements at Harrow get more regular injections of self-esteem and more building foods than we do at Mynydd Coch. We hear also that they do not go home at the end of each school day but sleep in the buildings and do not have two furlongs of uphill walking to get to their lessons, and that must be an advantage from the point of view of turning up fresh in the morning. We climb and a lot of us

get bent nearly double in the process, for whatever substance it is that keeps spines straight seems to find it easy to give up the ghost in this area.

That not only establishes a clear sense of place from the very start but signals also the social, spiritual and political preoccupations of the book and its characters, as well as introducing us to Thomas's florid prose style. 'Elements' was one of the two words he regularly employed to describe people in general: 'voters' was the other. In real life Mynydd Coch did not exist as a village but he borrowed the name of a hill in Powys, east of Dolgellau. He actually came from farther south, in the Rhondda valley, the youngest of twelve children whose father looked after the pit ponies in the local coal mine. His description of the fictional village as 'nothing more than a quadrangle of slopes, coal, rent and chaos', where life was 'bleak and confusing', must surely reflect his own childhood experience, embellished with the fruits of his extravagant imagination. Later, when visiting the house of a comparatively wealthy farmer, his narrator observes: 'The furniture in the room strikes us as remarkably solid, for there are few articles in Mynydd Coch meant to outlast a short generation or a stubborn bailiff.'

Thomas acknowledged the tradition of Nonconformism in Welsh villages by endowing Mynydd Coch with two rival sects. The Lookers are constantly on the watch for the first signs of Armageddon. As one of their number explains: 'The Lookers think there is no hope for man, the whole species being a corrupt lot of rodneys, that doom is whizzing towards them with a fierce light in its eye and an armful of destructive paraphernalia that will take the crease out of man's trousers for evermore.' (As his interlocutor remarks: 'I don't see how that clashes really with the broad principles of the Church.')

The other sect is the Drummers, whose founder Evan Jacobs once saw a cloud formation that looked like a hand cupped over an ear, persuading him that God is deaf. His followers bang their drums with gusto to attract His attention. 'If God was not deaf at the time that Evan saw the ear in the sky, it might well be true after 24 months of hard beating on the pig-skin by this body of Drummers.' We learn, too, that the historical research section of the school library contains little but the memoirs of Welsh preachers; and we are introduced to the League for the Protection of Young Girls, whose members are devoted to rooting out lust, principally by disrupting lovers' trysts.

Set in the early 1940s towards the end of the Second World War, *A Frost on My Frolic* has little in the way of an over-arching plot but is rather a series of comic incidents and catastrophes that climax in a surprisingly brutal ending. The victim of many misfortunes is Mr Rawlins, the teacher who runs most aspects of school life. When the collapse of several dining-tables in the newly equipped canteen finds him spattered with bits of food, we are told: 'All in all, he has never looked more like a chosen and anointed offspring of the force that arranges the neat seat of mankind's breeches in perfect readiness for marriage with the swinging toe-cap of disaster's patient pendulum.'

Thomas had lived through some of the most severe hits of disaster's pendulum in the Twenties and Thirties, when the closure of many Welsh pits provoked industrial unrest. This is reflected in the novel, as he describes the experience of two former miners who had taken part in the protests. One of them had started out as a fearless militant, whose face during demonstrations 'was always alight with a great joy'. That did not last, though.

> The movement began to falter and rust. The mine-owners beat us to a frazzle. It was a sullen, mad, mouldering sort of world we lived in when the last of the big strikes found us even nearer the grave than we had been before. Men like Lew Price were large enough to see the closing of collieries and the gutting of whole towns as nothing more than incidents in a struggle to which many more generations might yet have to be given up.

He led the first hunger marches to London and that hurried up the job the lung-dust had begun.

As the book progresses, such bleak reflections begin to crowd out the jokes. Rereading it after sixty-five years, I realized that I had forgotten the stark ending, the sting in the tail, and how it strikes a note that will grate with most readers today. It involves a rape whose perpetrator – the farmer with the nice furniture, as it turns out – gets away with it. Who's laughing now?

Writing novels was only one part of Thomas's eclectic life and occupied a relatively short period. The first of them, *The Dark Philosophers*, was published in 1946, the tenth and last, *The Love Man*, in 1958. After that he wrote some moderately successful plays – mainly for radio – and developed a new career as a witty television pundit, appearing quite often on the panel of *The Brains Trust*, which had moved from radio to TV in 1955. He also became a frequent contributor to *Punch*. All the same, it took him a while to acquire the confidence in his earning abilities that would allow him to give up the day job: he worked as a schoolteacher from 1940 until 1962.

His entry in the *Oxford Dictionary of National Biography* sums up his craft with insight and elegance: 'What disturbed and enthralled Thomas's readers was that the stuff of gritty realism and documentary melodrama was being shifted by hyperbolic wit and cascades of metaphor into a completely different mode: murderously savage in intent and relentlessly conscious that self-aware laughter is the only way the joker ever manages to be the judge.' He merits a renaissance.

MICHAEL LEAPMAN has written seventeen books, all non-fiction. They include a political biography of Neil Kinnock, which took him for the first time to the Welsh valleys that Gwyn Thomas wrote about. He has been a journalist for sixty years and still bursts into print from time to time.

Delivering a Missing Letter

KATE MORGAN

A disused bus shelter in the market town of Sedbergh is a curious place for a quest to end, literary or otherwise. The town itself is rather curious too; geographically in Cumbria but on the wrong side of the M6 to be in the Lake District proper, it sits almost exactly on the watershed where the rolling green fells give way to the harsher limestone uplands of the Yorkshire Dales. Hard up against the Howgill Fells, it has always attracted walkers but in recent years it has also become a haven for readers. It now has seven bookshops, including an enormous second-hand one at the end of the High Street, and bookshelves are squeezed into any available space in the town's other shops and cafés. When we arrived for cake and a potter while holidaying in Hawes, it was more in hope than expectation that here we would find the missing piece to complete the Scandinavian puzzle that our dining-room bookshelf had become.

Collecting books is a funny thing and not something I'd ever set out to do. I have multiple copies of *The Wind in the Willows* because it's an enduring favourite which I happen to misplace periodically and firmly believe should be on everyone's shelf, young or old. I have almost all of the *Poldark* novels by Winston Graham, but that's because I wanted to read them, not acquire them. The same goes in

---

Maj Sjöwall and Per Wahlöö, *Roseanna* (1965), *The Man Who Went up in Smoke* (1966), *The Man on the Balcony* (1967), *The Laughing Policeman* (1968), *The Fire Engine that Disappeared* (1969), *Murder at the Savoy* (1970), *The Abominable Man* (1971), *The Locked Room* (1972), *Cop Killer* (1974) and *The Terrorists* (1975) are all available as 4th Estate paperbacks, from £8.99 each.

our house for Jo Nesbo and Roddy Doyle. They've been collected because they've been read, not the other way around. Collecting books is the ultimate rejoinder to digital books, making the book itself a physical item to treasure as much as the words contained within. But books are not intended to be just placed on a shelf to be admired. Until they're taken down and opened, they're not really books at all.

Several years ago, my husband picked up a copy of a book called *Roseanna*, probably from an Oxfam bookshop. It was a detective story, in all senses of the phrase, set in 1960s Stockholm and featuring a Swedish policeman named Martin Beck. In it a young American tourist on a riverboat tour across Sweden is murdered, but the plot is secondary to a portrait of Martin Beck and the shortcomings of the police and the wider political system in which he is required to operate. We both read it, one after the other, even though our reading tastes rarely coincide. (I've never been tempted by his Irvine Welshes and he's always run a mile from my Jane Austens.) But on this one, we were agreed. It was rather good. And then we discovered that there were more – ten in all, written by a pair of journalists who happened to be both committed Marxists and husband and wife. Maj Sjöwall and Per Wahlöö conceived the entire Beck series as a story in ten chapters, which they created together, writing alternate chapters, over a ten-year period between 1965 and 1975.

On one level, the books are straightforward crime fiction. The stories are complex but not complicated, told in clean Nordic prose. Scandinavian crime fiction has conquered the world in the last few decades, but the Beck novels have been largely (possibly criminally) overlooked. They are not simply police procedurals, they are *the* police procedural which kick-started the entire genre. Written in an era before DNA came of age and when the Internet was still thirty years away, they strip back crime detection to its nuts and bolts. Beck's genes can be found in Kurt Wallander and Harry Hole, but his reach has gone far beyond Scandinavia. As a world-weary policeman with a social conscience, his influence can be found in any modern crime novel where the *whydunit* is just as important as the *who*.

It wasn't until we'd picked up a few more in the series that the collection really began in earnest. As good as the books are, I have to admit that the urge to collect was sparked by other considerations. The copy of *Roseanna* that had started things off was a Harper Perennial edition from 2007 and on the spine of the book was the title in a spare oblong font, above which were the letter M and the numeral 1. Arrayed in order, the spines of the ten books would spell out MARTIN BECK. By this point, we had picked up a few in no particular order, and it was uniquely frustrating to look at the shelf and see just MTNB. There was nothing else for it. We had to complete the set.

Browsing in bookshops is hardly a chore and I've even planned entire weekends away around it, but the thrill of the chase gave our mooching an added sense of purpose. The peerless Barter Books in Alnwick yielded two, *Cop Killer* and *The Terrorists*, which we celebrated with cheese toasties in front of the fire in the station buffet. *The Laughing Policeman*, probably my favourite of the ten, turned up on a post-Christmas break to Lyme Regis, in a tiny honesty bookshop set back from the bustle of the harbour. We dropped a pound in the box and noted what we'd taken in the reporter's notebook that served as a stock control system, then walked out to look back at the town in late December sunshine from the end of the Cobb. Like any good treasure hunt, there were surprises along the way. We returned empty-handed from an expedition to Hay one August bank holiday but tracked down the second book of the series in a Cannock charity shop on a miserable January lunchtime.

Eventually, the bookshelf proclaimed MARTINBCK and we had only to find the eighth book. Beck novels were suddenly everywhere but they were always numbers one or nine or four. When we came to Sedbergh, we hoped to find it in one of the town's bookshops but we didn't dream it would find us. Walking along the High Street, we spotted a defunct bus stop which had been repurposed as a Book Shelter. It was now lined with bookshelves instead of timetables, the idea being that you could borrow and return a book or swap one from the Shelter for one of your own. From several paces away, we could see the distinctive spine of a Beck and, nostrils twitching in anticipation, we came closer. There it was – *The Locked Room*, the elusive eighth book. Reflecting on the cosmic coincidences that had led to that book being deposited on that shelf in time for our arrival, I very nearly fell on my knees in the middle of the street.

As the whole system worked on an exchange principle, we couldn't just take it and so I dashed into the charity bookshop across the road to buy a suitable offering to the Book gods that had brought us and the book to Sedbergh at this very moment. We'd visited Haworth the day before, and in the fields behind the Parsonage I'd seen four Japanese girls, clearly on a pilgrimage. They were waving scarves and dancing in a circle, looking as if they were trying to summon the spirit of Emily or Anne, or perhaps even Cathy's ghost. So a well-thumbed copy of *Jane Eyre* seemed an appropriate replacement. We toasted the end of the quest with swift halves in the Black Bull and made plans to return to dine there one day.

When we slotted E into place, I half-expected the bookshelf to slide creakily open to reveal a secret staircase. It didn't, of course. But the conclusion of our hunt has left its mark in other ways. We still reflexively look to the 'S' or 'W' shelf as soon as we enter a bookshop and always point out a Beck book when we see one out of sheer instinct. The act of searching them out often led to unexpected shared delights, finding other bookish treasures or a newly discovered bookshop that we might otherwise have walked past. We've both yet to read the final book in the series, as that will truly mark the end of our adventure. Of course, we could have ordered the lot from Amazon in one go and filled the shelf in a matter of days. But where would have been the fun in that?

KATE MORGAN used to fill her time between bookshop jaunts by working as a lawyer. She is now a university law lecturer in Birmingham and is also working on her first book.

Bibliography

Coming attractions

SAM LEITH is unsettled by Ray Bradbury · AMANDA THEUNISSEN visits Trebizond with Aunt Dot · NIGEL ANDREW attends a country wedding · URSULA BUCHAN helps out at her local library · ANTHONY LONGDEN is fascinated by the story of a fire foretold · SUE GEE finds inspiration in bookmarks · ADAM SISMAN goes back to *Middlemarch* · CLARISSA BURDEN enjoys the company of a very dapper detective · CHRIS SAUNDERS goes tramping